CRIMES
OF THE HEART

BY BETH HENLEY

DRAMATISTS
PLAY SERVICE
INC.

CRIMES OF THE HEART
Copyright © 1982, Beth Henley
Copyright © 1981, Beth Henley
as an unpublished dramatic composition

All Rights Reserved

SPECIAL NOTE

Originally produced by the Actors Theatre of Louisville, Inc., in February 1979.

CRIMES OF THE HEART received its New York Premiere
at the Manhattan Theatre Club in 1980.

Produced on the Broadway Stage by Warner Theatre Productions, Inc./Claire Nichtern,
Mary Lea Johnson, Martin Richards, Francine Lefrak.

CRIMES OF THE HEART was presented on Broadway by Warner Theatre Productions, Inc./Claire Nichtern, Mary Lea Johnson, Martin Richards, and Francine Lefrak, at the Golden Theatre, in New York City, on November 4, 1981. It was directed by Melvin Bernhardt; the set was by John Lee Beatty; costumes were by Patricia McGourty; and the lighting was by Dennis Parichy. The associate producer was Ethel Watt. The cast, in order of appearance, was as follows:

LENNY MAGRATH .... Lizbeth Mackay
CHICK BOYLE .... Sharon Ullrick
DOC PORTER .... Raymond Baker
MEG MAGRATH .... Mary Beth Hurt
BABE BOTRELLE .... Mia Dillon
BARNETTE LLOYD .... Peter MacNicol

CRIMES OF THE HEART received its New York premiere at the Manhattan Theatre Club, in 1980.

Originally produced by Actors Theatre of Louisville, Inc. in February, 1979.

"For Len, C.C., and Kayo."

THE CAST

LENNY MAGRATH, 30, the oldest sister
CHICK BOYLE, 29, the sisters' first cousin
DOC PORTER, 30, Meg's old boyfriend
MEG MAGRATH, 27, the middle sister
BABE BOTRELLE, 24, the youngest sister
BARNETTE LLOYD, 26, Babe's lawyer

THE SETTING

The setting of the entire play is the kitchen in the Magrath sisters' house in Hazlehurst, Mississippi, a small southern town. The old-fashioned kitchen is unusually spacious, but there is a lived-in cluttered look about it. There are four different entrances and exits to the kitchen: the back door; the door leading to the dining room and the front of the house; a door leading to the downstairs bedroom; and a staircase leading to the upstairs room. There is a table near the center of the room, and a cot has been set up in one of the corners.

THE TIME

In the fall; five years after Hurricane Camille

CRIMES OF THE HEART

ACT I

The lights go up on the empty kitchen. It is late afternoon. Lenny Magrath, a thirty-year-old woman with a round figure and face, enters from the back door carrying a white suitcase, a saxophone case, and a brown paper sack. She sets the suitcase and the sax case down and takes the brown sack to the kitchen table. After glancing quickly at the door, she gets the cookie jar from the kitchen counter, a box of matches from the stove and then brings both objects back down to the kitchen table. Excitedly, she reaches into the brown sack and pulls out a package of birthday candles. She quickly opens the package and removes a candle. She tries to stick the candle into a cookie— it falls off. She sticks the candle in again but the cookie is too hard and it crumbles. Frantically, she gets a second cookie from the jar. She strikes a match, lights the candle and begins dripping wax onto the cookie. Just as she is beginning to smile we hear Chick's voice from Offstage.

CHICK'S VOICE. Lenny! Oh, Lenny! (*Lenny quickly blows out the candle and stuffs the cookie and candle into her dress pocket. Chick, 29, enters from the back door. She is a brightly dressed matron with yellow hair and shiny, red lips.*)
CHICK. Hi! I saw your car pull up.
LENNY. Hi.
CHICK. Well, did you see today's paper? (*Lenny nods.*) It's

just too awful! It's just way too awful! How I'm gonna continue holding my head up high in this community, I do not know. Did you remember to pick up those pantyhose for me?

LENNY. They're in the sack.

CHICK. Well, thank goodness, at least I'm not gonna have to go into town wearing holes in my stockings. (*Chick gets the package, tears it open and proceeds to take off one pair of stockings and put on another, throughout the following scene. There should be something slightly grotesque about this woman changing her stockings in the kitchen.*)

LENNY. Did Uncle Watson call?

CHICK. Yes, Daddy has called me twice already. He said Babe's ready to come home. We've got to get right over and pick her up before they change their simple minds.

LENNY. (*Hesitantly.*) Oh, I know, of course, it's just—

CHICK. What?

LENNY. Well, I was hoping Meg would call.

CHICK. Meg?

LENNY. Yes, I sent her a telegram: about Babe, and—

CHICK. A telegram?! Couldn't you just phone her up?

LENNY. Well, no, 'cause her phone's ... out of order.

CHICK. Out of order?

LENNY. Disconnected. I don't know what.

CHICK. Well, that sounds like Meg. My, these are snug. Are you sure you bought my right size?

LENNY. (*Looking at the box.*) Size extra petite.

CHICK. Well, they're skimping on the nylon material. (*Struggling to pull up the stockings.*) That's all there is to it. Skimping on the nylon. (*She finishes on one leg and starts on the other.*) Now, just what all did you say in this "telegram" to Meg?

LENNY. I don't recall exactly. I, well, I just told her to come on home.

CHICK. To come on home! Why, Lenora Josephine, have you lost your only brain, or what?

LENNY. (*Nervously, as she begins to pick up the mess of dirty stockings and plastic wrappings.*) But Babe wants Meg home. She asked me to call her.

CHICK. I'm not talking about what Babe wants.

6

LENNY. Well, what then?

CHICK. Listen, Lenora, I think it's pretty accurate to assume that after this morning's paper, Babe's gonna be incurring some mighty negative publicity around this town. And Meg's appearance isn't gonna help out a bit.

LENNY. What's wrong with Meg?

CHICK. She had a loose reputation in high school.

LENNY. (*Weakly.*) She was popular.

CHICK. She was known all over Copiah County as cheap Christmas trash, and that was the least of it. There was that whole sordid affair with Doc Porter, leaving him a cripple.

LENNY. A cripple—he's got a limp. Just, kind of, barely a limp.

CHICK. Well, his mother was going to keep *me* out of the Ladies' Social League because of it.

LENNY. What?

CHICK. That's right. I never told you, but I had to go plead with that mean, old woman and convince her that I was just as appalled and upset with what Meg had done as she was, and that I was only a first cousin anyway and I could hardly be blamed for all the skeletons in the Magraths' closet. It was humiliating. I tell you, she even brought up your mother's death. And that poor cat.

LENNY. Oh! Oh! Oh, please, Chick! I'm sorry. But you're in the Ladies' League now.

CHICK. Yes. That's true, I am. But frankly, if Mrs. Porter hadn't developed tha: tumor in her bladder, I wouldn't be in the club today, much less a committee head. (*As she brushes her hair.*) Anyway, you be a sweet potato and wait right here for Meg to call, so's you can convince her not to come back home. It would make things a whole lot easier on everybody. Don't you think it really would?

LENNY. Probably.

CHICK. Good, then suit yourself. How's my hair?

LENNY. Fine.

CHICK. Not pooching out in the back, is it?

LENNY. No.

CHICK. (*Cleaning the hair from her brush.*) All right then, I'm on my way. I've got Annie May over there keeping an eye on

Peekay and Buck Jr., but I don't trust her with them for long periods of time. (*Dropping the ball of hair onto the floor.*) Her mind is like a loose sieve. Honestly it is. (*She puts the brush back into her purse.*) Oh! Oh! Oh! I almost forgot. Here's a present for you. Happy Birthday to Lenny, from the Buck Boyles! (*Chick takes a wrapped package from her bag and hands it to Lenny.*)

LENNY. Why, thank you, Chick. It's so nice to have your remember my birthday every year like you do.

CHICK. (*Modestly.*) Oh well, now, that's just the way I am, I suppose. That's just the way I was brought up to be. Well, why don't you go on and open up the present?

LENNY. All right. (*She starts to unwrap the gift.*)

CHICK. It's a box of candy—assorted cremes.

LENNY. Candy—that's always a nice gift.

CHICK. And you have a sweet tooth, don't you?

LENNY. I guess.

CHICK. Well, I'm glad you like it.

LENNY. I do.

CHICK. Oh, speaking of which, remember that little polka dot dress you got Peekay for her fifth birthday last month?

LENNY. The red and white one?

CHICK. Yes; well, the first time I put it in the washing machine, I mean the very first time, it fell all to pieces. Those little polka dots just dropped right off in the water.

LENNY. (*Crushed.*) Oh, no. Well, I'll get something else for her then—a little toy.

CHICK. Oh, no, no, no, no, no! We wouldn't hear of it! I just wanted to let you know so you wouldn't go and waste any more of your hard-earned money on that make of dress. Those inexpensive brands just don't hold up. I'm sorry but not in these modern washing machines.

DOC PORTER'S VOICE. Hello! Hello, Lenny!

CHICK. (*Taking over.*) Oh, look, it's Doc Porter! Come on in, Doc! Please come right on in! (*Doc Porter enters through the back door. He is carrying a large sack of pecans. Doc is an attractively worn man with a slight limp that adds rather than detracts from his quiet seductive quality. He is 30 years old,*

8

but appears slightly older.) Well, how are you doing? How in the world are you doing?

DOC. Just fine, Chick.

CHICK. And how are you liking it now that you're back in Hazle-hurst?

DOC. Oh, I'm finding it somewhat enjoyable.

CHICK. Somewhat! Only somewhat! Will you listen to him! What a silly, silly, silly man! Well, I'm on my way. I've got some people waiting on me. (*Whispering to Doc.*) It's Babe. I'm on my way to pick her up.

DOC. Oh.

CHICK. Well, goodbye! Farewell and goodbye!

LENNY. Bye. (*Chick exits.*)

DOC. Hello.

LENNY. Hi. I guess you heard about the thing with Babe.

DOC. Yeah.

LENNY. It was in the newspaper.

DOC. Uh huh.

LENNY. What a mess.

DOC. Yeah.

LENNY. Well, come on and sit down. I'll heat us up some coffee.

DOC. That's okay. I can only stay a minute. I have to pick up Scott; he's at the dentist's.

LENNY. Oh; well, I'll heat some up for myself. I'm kinda thirsty for a cup of hot coffee. (*Lenny puts the coffeepot on the burner.*)

DOC. Lenny—

LENNY. What?

DOC. (*Not able to go on.*) Ah . . .

LENNY. Yes?

DOC. Here, some pecans for you. (*He hands her the sack.*)

LENNY. Why, thank you, Doc. I love pecans.

DOC. My wife and Scott picked them up around the yard.

LENNY. Well, I can use them to make a pie. A pecan pie.

DOC. Yeah. Look, Lenny, I've got some bad news for you.

LENNY. What?

DOC. Well, you know, you've been keeping Billy Boy out on our farm; he's been grazing out there.

LENNY. Yes—

9

DOC. Well, last night, Billy Boy died.

LENNY. He died?

DOC. Yeah. I'm sorry to tell you when you've got all this on you; but I thought you'd want to know.

LENNY. Well, yeah. I do. He died?

DOC. Uh huh. He was struck by lightning.

LENNY. Struck by lightning? In that storm yesterday?

DOC. That's what we think.

LENNY. Gosh, struck by lightning. I've had Billy Boy so long. You know. Ever since I was ten years old.

DOC. Yeah. He was a mighty old horse.

LENNY. (*Stung.*) Mighty old.

DOC. Almost twenty years old.

LENNY. That's right, twenty years. 'Cause; ah; I'm thirty years old today. Did you know that?

DOC. No, Lenny, I didn't know. Happy Birthday.

LENNY. Thanks. (*She begins to cry.*)

DOC. Oh, come on now, Lenny. Come on. Hey, hey, now. You know I can't stand it when you Magrath women start to cry. You know it just gets me.

LENNY. Oh-ho! Sure! You mean when Meg cries! Meg's the one you could never stand to watch cry! Not me! I could fill up a pig's trough!

DOC. Now, Lenny ... stop it. Come on. Jesus!

LENNY. Okay! Okay! I don't know what's wrong with me. I don't mean to make a scene. I've been on this crying jag. (*She blows her nose.*) All this stuff with Babe and old Granddaddy's gotten worse in the hospital and I can't get in touch with Meg.

DOC. You tried calling Meggy?

LENNY. Yes.

DOC. Is she coming home?

LENNY. Who knows. She hasn't called me. That's what I'm waiting here for—hoping she'll call.

DOC. She still living in California?

LENNY. Yes; in Hollywood.

DOC. Well, give me a call if she gets in. I'd like to see her.

LENNY. Oh, you would, huh?

DOC. Yeah, Lenny, sad to say, but I would.

10

LENNY. It is sad. It's very sad indeed. (*They stare at each other, then look away. There is a moment of tense silence.*)
DOC. Hey, Jello Face, your coffee's boiling.
LENNY. (*Going to check.*) Oh, it is? Thanks. (*After she checks the pot.*) Look, you'd better go on and pick Scott up. You don't want him to have to wait for you.
DOC. Yeah, you're right. Poor kid. It's his first time at the dentist.
LENNY. Poor thing.
DOC. Well, 'bye. I'm sorry to have to tell you about your horse.
LENNY. Oh, I know. Tell Joan thanks for picking up the pecans.
DOC. I will. (*He starts to leave.*)
LENNY. Oh, how's the baby?
DOC. She's fine. Real pretty. She, ah, holds your finger in her hand; like this.
LENNY. Oh, that's cute.
DOC. Yeah. 'Bye, Lenny.
LENNY. 'Bye. (*Doc exits. Lenny stares after him for a moment, then goes and sits back down at the kitchen table. She reaches into her pocket and pulls out a somewhat crumbled cookie and a wax candle. She lights the candle again, lets the wax drip onto the cookie, then sticks the candle on top of the cookie. She begins to sing the "Happy Birthday Song" to herself. At the end of the song she pauses, silently makes a wish, and blows out the candle. She waits a moment, then re-lights the candle, and repeats her actions, only this time making a different wish at the end of the song. She starts to repeat the procedure for the third time, as the phone begins to ring. She goes to answer it.*) Hello . . . oh, hello, Lucille, how's Zackery? . . . Oh, no! . . . Oh, I'm so sorry. Of course, it must be grueling for you . . . Yes, I understand. Your only brother . . . no, she's not here yet. Chick just went to pick her up . . . oh, now, Lucille, she's still his wife, I'm sure she'll be interested . . . Well, you can just tell me the information and I'll relate it all to her . . . Uh-hum, his liver's saved. Oh, that's good news! . . . Well, of course, when you look at it like that . . . Breathing stabilized . . . Damage to the spinal column, not yet determined . . . Okay . . . Yes, Lucille, I've got it all down . . . Uh-huh, I'll give her that message. 'Bye, 'bye.

(*Lenny drops the pencil and paper down. She sighs deeply, wipes her cheeks with the back of her hand, and goes to the stove to pour herself a cup of coffee. After a few moments, the front door is heard slamming. Lenny starts. A whistle is heard, then Meg's voice.*)

MEG'S VOICE. I'm home! (*She whistles the family whistle.*) Anybody home?!!

LENNY. Meg? Meg! (*Meg, 27, enters from the dining room. She has sad, magic eyes and wears a hat. She carries a worn-out suitcase.*)

MEG. (*Dropping her suitcase, running to hug Lenny.*) Lenny—

LENNY. Well, Meg! Why, Meg! Oh, Meggy! Why didn't you call? Did you fly in? You didn't take a cab, did you? Why didn't you give us a call?

MEG. (*Overlapping.*) Oh, Lenny! Why, Lenny! Dear, Lenny! (*Then she looks at Lenny's face.*) My God, we're getting so old! Oh, I called for heaven's sake. Of course, I called!

LENNY. Well, I never talked to you—

MEG. Well, I know! I let the phone ring right off the hook!

LENNY. Well, as a matter of fact, I was out most of the morning seeing to Babe—!

MEG. Now just what's all this business about Babe? How could you send me such a telegram about Babe? And Zackery! You say somebody's shot Zackery?!

LENNY. Yes; they have.

MEG. Well, good Lord! Is he dead?

LENNY. No. But he's in the hospital. He was shot in his stomach.

MEG. In his stomach! How awful! Do they know who shot him? (*Lenny nods.*) Well, who? Who was it? Who? Who?

LENNY. Babe! They're all saying Babe shot him! They took her to jail! And they're saying she shot him! They're all saying it! It's horrible! It's awful!

MEG. (*Overlapping.*) Jail! Good Lord, jail! Well, who? Who's saying it? Who?!!

LENNY. Everyone!! The policemen, the sheriff, Zackery, even Babe's saying it! Even Babe herself!!

MEG. Well, for God's sake. For God's sake.

12

LENNY. (*Overlapping as she falls apart.*) It's horrible! It's horrible! It's just horrible!!!

MEG. Now calm down, Lenny. Just calm down. Would you like a Coke? Here, I'll get you some Coke. (*Meg gets a Coke from the refrigerator. She opens it and downs a large swig.*) Why? Why would she shoot him? Why? (*Meg hands the Coke bottle to Lenny.*)

LENNY. I talked to her this morning and I asked her that very question. I said, "Babe, why would you shoot Zackery? He was your own husband. Why would you shoot him?" And do you know what she said? (*Meg shakes her head.*) She said, "Cause I didn't like his looks. I just didn't like his looks."

MEG. (*After a pause.*) Well, I don't like his looks.

LENNY. But you didn't shoot him! You wouldn't shoot a person 'cause you didn't like their looks! You wouldn't do that! Oh, I hate to say this—I do hate to say this—but I believe Babe is ill. I mean in-her-head-ill.

MEG. Oh, now, Lenny, don't you say that! There're plenty of good sane reasons to shoot another person and I'm sure that Babe had one. Now what we've got to do is get her the best lawyer in town. Do you have any ideas on who's the best lawyer in town?

LENNY. Well, Zackery is, of course; but he's been shot!

MEG. Well, count him out! Just count him and his whole firm out!

LENNY. Anyway, you don't have to worry, she's already got her lawyer.

MEG. She does? Who?

LENNY. Barnette Lloyd. Annie Lloyd's boy. He just opened his office here in town. And Uncle Watson said we'd be doing Annie a favor by hiring him up.

MEG. Doing Annie a favor? Doing Annie a favor?! Well, what about Babe? Have you thought about Babe? Do we want to do her a favor of thirty or forty years in jail?! Have you thought about that?

LENNY. Now, don't snap at me! Just don't snap at me! I try to do what's right! All this responsibility keeps falling on my shoulders, and I try to do what's right!

13

MEG. Well, boo hoo, hoo, hoo! And how in the hell could you send me such a telegram about Babe!

LENNY. Well, if you had a phone, or if you didn't live way out there in Hollywood and not even come home for Christmas maybe I wouldn't have to pay all that money to send you a telegram!!!

MEG. (*Overlapping.*) 'Babe's in terrible trouble—Stop! Zackery's been shot—Stop! Come home immediately—Stop! Stop! Stop!'

LENNY. And what was that you said about how old we're getting? When you looked at my face, you said, "My God, we're getting so old!" But you didn't mean we—you meant me! Didn't you? I'm thirty years old today and my face is getting all pinched up and my hair is falling out in the comb.

MEG. Why, Lenny! It's your birthday, October 23rd. How could I forget. Happy Birthday!

LENNY. Well, it's not. I'm thirty years old and Billy Boy died last night. He was struck by lightning. He was struck dead.

MEG. (*Reaching for a cigarette.*) Struck dead. Oh, what a mess. What a mess. Are you really thirty? Then I must be twenty-seven and Babe is twenty-four. My God, we're getting so old. (*They are silent for several moments as Meg drags off her cigarette and Lenny drinks her Coke.*) What's the cot doing in the kitchen?

LENNY. Well, I rolled it out when Old Granddaddy got sick. So I could be close and hear him at night if he needed something.

MEG. (*Glancing toward the door leading to the downstairs bedroom.*) Is Old Granddaddy here?

LENNY. Why, no. Old Granddaddy's at the hospital.

MEG. Again?

LENNY. Meg!

MEG. What?

LENNY. I wrote you all about it. He's been in the hospital over three months straight.

MEG. He has?

LENNY. Don't you remember? I wrote you about all those blood vessels popping in his brain?

MEG. Popping—

14

LENNY. And how he was so anxious to hear from you and to find out about your singing career. I wrote it all to you. How they have to feed him through those tubes now. Didn't you get my letters?

MEG. Oh, I don't know, Lenny. I guess I did. To tell you the truth, sometimes I kinda don't read your letters.

LENNY. What?

MEG. I'm sorry. I used to read them. It's just since Christmas reading them gives me these slicing pains right here in my chest.

LENNY. I see. I see. Is that why you didn't use that money Old Granddaddy sent you to come home Christmas; because you hate us so much? We never did all that much to make you hate us. We didn't!

MEG. Oh, Lenny! Do you think I'd be getting slicing pains in my chest, if I didn't care about you?! If I hated you? Honestly, now, do you think I would?

LENNY. No.

MEG. Okay, then. Let's drop it. I'm sorry I didn't read your letters. Okay?

LENNY. Okay.

MEG. Anyway, we've got this whole thing with Babe to deal with. The first thing is to get her a good lawyer and get her out of jail.

LENNY. Well, she's out of jail.

MEG. She is?

LENNY. That young lawyer, he's gotten her out.

MEG. Oh, he has?

LENNY. Yes, on bail. Uncle Watson's put it up. Chick's bringing her back right now—she's driving her home.

MEG. Oh; well, that's a relief.

LENNY. Yes, and they're due home any minute now; so we can just wait right here for 'em.

MEG. Well, good. That's good. (*As she leans against the counter.*) So, Babe shot Zackery Botrelle, the richest and most powerful man in all of Hazlehurst, slap in the gut. It's hard to believe.

LENNY. It certainly is. Little Babe—shooting off a gun.

MEG. Little Babe.

LENNY. She was always the prettiest and most perfect of the

15

three of us. Old Granddaddy used to call her his Dancing Sugar Plum. Why, remember how proud and happy he was the day she married Zackery.

MEG. Yes, I remember. It was his finest hour.

LENNY. He remarked how Babe was gonna skyrocket right to the heights of Hazlehurst society. And how Zackery was just the right man for her whether she knew it now or not.

MEG. Oh, Lordy, Lordy. And what does Old Granddaddy say now?

LENNY. Well, I haven't had the courage to tell him all about this as yet. I thought maybe tonight we could go to visit him at the hospital and you could talk to him and . . .

MEG. Yeah, well, we'll see. We'll see. Do we have anything to drink around here—to the tune of straight bourbon?

LENNY. No. There's no liquor.

MEG. Hell. (*Meg gets a Coke from the refrigerator and opens it.*)

LENNY. Then you will go with me to see Old Granddaddy at the hospital tonight?

MEG. Of course. (*Meg goes to her purse and gets out a bottle of Empirin Compound. She takes out a tablet and puts it on her tongue.*) Brother, I know he's gonna go on about my singing career. Just like he always does.

LENNY. Well, how is your career going?

MEG. It's not.

LENNY. Why, aren't you still singing at that club down on Malibu beach?

MEG. No. Not since Christmas.

LENNY. Well, then, are you singing some place new?

MEG. No, I'm not singing. I'm not singing at all.

LENNY. Oh. Well, what do you do then?

MEG. What I do is I pay cold storage bills for a dog food company. That's what I do.

LENNY. (*Trying to be helpful.*) Gosh, don't you think it'd be a good idea to stay in the show business field?

MEG. Oh, maybe.

LENNY. Like Old Granddaddy says, "With your talent all you need is exposure. Then you can make your own breaks!" Did you hear his suggestion about getting your foot put in one of those blocks of cement they've got out there? He thinks that's real important.

MEG. Yeh. I think I've heard that. And I'll probably hear it again when I go to visit him at the hospital tonight; so let's just drop it. Okay? (*She notices the sack of pecans.*) What's this? Pecans? Great, I love pecans! (*Meg takes out two pecans and tries to open them by cracking them together.*) Come on... Crack, you demons! Crack!

LENNY. We have a nutcracker!

MEG. (*Trying with her teeth.*) Ah, where's the sport in a nutcracker? Where's the challenge?

LENNY. (*Getting up to get the nutcracker.*) It's over here in the utensil drawer. (*As Lenny gets the nutcracker, Meg opens the pecan by stepping on it with her shoe.*)

MEG. There! Open! (*Meg picks up the crumbled pecan and eats it.*) Mmmm, delicious. Delicious. Where'd you get the fresh pecans?

LENNY. Oh...I don't know.

MEG. They sure are tasty.

LENNY. Doc Porter brought them over.

MEG. Doc. What's Doc doing here in town?

LENNY. Well, his father died a couple of months ago. Now he's back home seeing to his property.

MEG. Gosh, the last I heard of Doc, he was up in the East painting the walls of houses to earn a living. (*Amused.*) Heard he was living with some Yankee woman who made clay pots.

LENNY. Joan.

MEG. What?

LENNY. Her name's Joan. She came down here with him. That's one of her pots. Doc's married to her.

MEG. Married—

LENNY. Uh huh.

MEG. Doc married a Yankee?

LENNY. That's right; and they've got two kids.

MEG. Kids—

LENNY. A boy and a girl.

MEG. God. Then his kids must be half-Yankee.

17

LENNY. I suppose.

MEG. God. That really gets me. I don't know why, but somehow that really gets me.

LENNY. I don't know why it should.

MEG. And what a stupid-looking pot! Who'd buy it anyway?

LENNY. Wait—I think that's them. Yeah, that's Chick's car! Oh, there's Babe! Hello, Babe! They're home, Meg! They're home. (*Meg hides.*)

BABE'S VOICE. Lenny! I'm home! I'm free! (*Babe, 24, enters exuberantly. She has an angelic face and fierce, volatile eyes. She carries a pink pocketbook.*) I'm home! (*Meg jumps out of hiding.*) Oh, Meg—Look, it's Meg! (*Running to hug her.*) Meg! When did you get home?

MEG. Just now!

BABE. Well, it's so good to see you! I'm so glad you're home! I'm so relieved. (*Chick enters.*)

MEG. Why, Chick; hello.

CHICK. Hello, Cousin Margaret. What brings you back to Hazlehurst?

MEG. Oh, I came on home... (*Turning to Babe.*) I came on home to see about Babe.

BABE. (*Running to hug Meg.*) Oh, Meg—

MEG. How are things with you, Babe?

CHICK. Well, they are dismal, if you want my opinion. She is refusing to cooperate with her lawyer, that nice-looking young Lloyd boy. She won't tell any of us why she committed this heinous crime, except to say that she didn't like Zackery's looks—

BABE. Oh, look, Lenny brought my suitcase from home! And my saxophone! Thank you! (*Babe runs over to the cot and gets out her saxophone.*)

CHICK. Now that young lawyer is coming over here this afternoon, and when he gets here he expects to get some concrete answers! That's what he expects! No more of this nonsense and stubbornness from you, Rebecca Magrath, or they'll put you in jail and throw away the key!

BABE. Meg, come look at my new saxophone. I went to Jackson and bought it used. Feel it. It's so heavy.

MEG. It's beautiful. (*The room goes silent*)

18

CHICK. Isn't that right, won't they throw away the key?

LENNY. Well, honestly, I don't know about that—

CHICK. They will! And leave you there to rot. So, Rebecca, what are you going to tell Mr. Lloyd about shooting Zackery when he gets here? What are your reasons going to be?

BABE. (*Glaring.*) That I didn't like his looks! I just didn't like his stinking looks! And I don't like yours much either, Chick-the-Stick! So, just leave me alone! I mean it! Leave me alone! Oooh! (*Babe exits up the stairs. There is a long moment of silence.*)

CHICK. Well, I was only trying to warn her that she's going to have to help herself. It's just that she doesn't understand how serious the situation is. Does she? She doesn't have the vaguest idea. Does she now?

LENNY. Well, it's true, she does seem a little confused.

CHICK. And that's putting it mildly, Lenny honey. That's putting it mighty mild. So, Margaret, how's your singing career going? We keep looking for your picture in the movie magazines. (*Meg moves to light a cigarette.*) You know, you shouldn't smoke. It causes cancer. Cancer of the lungs. They say each cigarette is just a little stick of cancer. A little death stick.

MEG. That's what I like about it, Chick—taking a drag off of death. (*Meg takes a long, deep drag.*) Mmm! Gives me a sense of controlling my own destiny. What power! What exhilaration! Want a drag?

LENNY. (*Trying to break the tension.*) Ah, Zackery's liver's been saved! His sister called up and said his liver was saved. Isn't that good news?

MEG. Well, yes, that's fine news. Mighty fine news. Why I've been told that the liver's a powerful important bodily organ. I believe it's used to absorb all of our excess bile.

LENNY. Yes—well—it's been saved. (*The phone rings. Lenny gets it.*)

MEG. So! Did you hear all that good news about the liver, Little Chicken?

CHICK. I heard it. And don't you call me Chicken! (*Meg clucks like a chicken.*) I've told you a hundred times if I've told you once not to call me Chicken. You cannot call me Chicken.

LENNY. ...Oh, no! ...Of course, we'll be right over! 'Bye! (*She hangs up the phone.*) That was Annie May—Peekay and Buck Jr. have eaten paints!

CHICK. Oh, no! Are they all right? They're not sick? They're not sick, are they?!

LENNY. I don't know. I don't know. Come on. We've got to run on next door.

CHICK. (*Overlapping.*) Oh, God! Oh, please!! Please let them be all right! Don't let them die!! Please, don't let them die!! (*Chick runs Off howling with Lenny following after. Meg sits alone, finishing her cigarette. After a moment, Babe's voice is heard.*)

BABE'S VOICE. Pst—Psst! (*Meg looks around. Babe comes tiptoeing down the stairs.*)

BABE. Has she gone?

MEG. She's gone. Peekay and Buck Jr. just ate their paints.

BABE. What idiots.

MEG. Yeah.

BABE. You know, Chick's hated us ever since we had to mov here from Vicksburg to live with Old Grandmama and Old Grand-daddy.

MEG. She's an idiot.

BABE. Yeah. Do you know what she told me this morning while I was still behind bars and couldn't get away?

MEG. What?

BABE. She told me how embarrassing it was for her all those years ago, you know, when mama—

MEG. Yeah, down in the cellar.

BABE. She said our mama had shamed the entire family, and we were known notoriously all through Hazlehurst. (*About to cry.*) Then she went on to say how I would now be getting just as much bad publicity and humiliating her and the family all over again.

MEG. Ah, forget it, Babe. Just forget it.

BABE. I told her, "Mama got national coverage! National!" And if Zackery wasn't a senator from Copiah County, I probably wouldn't even be getting state-wide.

MEG. Of course you wouldn't.

BABE. (*After a pause.*) Gosh, sometimes I wonder . . .
MEG. What?
BABE. Why she did it. Why mama hung herself.
MEG. I don't know. She had a bad day. A real bad day. You know how it feels on a real bad day.
BABE. And that old yellow cat. It was sad about that old cat.
MEG. Yeah.
BABE. I bet if Daddy hadn't of left us, they'd still be alive.
MEG. Oh, I don't know.
BABE. 'Cause it was after he left that she started spending whole days just sitting there and smoking on the back porch steps. She'd sling her ashes down onto the different bugs and ants that'd be passing by.
MEG. Yeah. Well, I'm glad he left.
BABE. That old yellow cat'd stay back there with her.
MEG. God, he was a bastard.
BABE. I thought if she felt something for anyone it woulda been that old cat. Guess I musta been mistaken.
MEG. Really, with his white teeth, Daddy was such a bastard.
BABE. Was he? I don't remember. (*Meg blows out a mouthful of smoke. After a moment, uneasily.*) I think I'm gonna make some lemonade. You want some?
MEG. Sure. (*Babe cuts lemons, dumps sugar, stirs ice cubes, etc. throughout the following exchange.*) Babe. Why won't you talk? Why won't you tell anyone about shooting Zackery?
BABE. Oooh—
MEG. Why not? You must have had a good reason. Didn't you?
BABE. I guess I did.
MEG. Well, what was it?
BABE. I . . . I can't say.
MEG. Why not? (*Pause.*) Babe, why not? You can tell me.
BABE. 'Cause . . . I'm sort of . . . protecting someone.
MEG. Protecting someone? Oh, Babe, then you really didn't shoot him?! I knew you couldn't have done it!! I knew it!!!
BABE. No, I shot him. I shot him all right. I meant to kill him. I was aiming for his heart, but I guess my hands were shaking and I—just got him in the stomach.
MEG. (*Collapsing.*) I see.

BABE. (*Stirring the lemonade.*) So I'm guilty. And I'm just gonna have to take my punishment and go on to jail.

MEG. Oh, Babe—

BABE. Don't worry, Meg, jail's gonna be a relief to me. I can learn to play my new saxophone. I won't have to live with Zackery anymore. And I won't have his snoopy old sister, Lucille, coming over and pushing me around. Jail will be a relief. Here's your lemonade.

MEG. Thanks.

BABE. It taste okay?

MEG. Perfect.

BABE. I like a lot of sugar in mine. I'm gonna add some more sugar. (*Babe goes to add more sugar to her lemonade, as Lenny bursts through the back door in a state of excitement and confusion.*)

LENNY. Well, it looks like the paint is primarily on their arms and faces; but Chick wants me to drive them all over to Doctor Winn's just to make sure. (*Lenny grabs her car keys off of the counter and as she does so, she notices the mess of lemons and sugar.*) Oh, now, Babe, try not to make a mess here; and be careful with this sharp knife. Honestly, all that sugar's gonna get you sick. Well, 'bye, 'bye. I'll be back as soon as I can.

MEG. 'Bye, Lenny.

BABE. 'Bye. (*Lenny exits.*) Boy, I don't know what's happening to Lenny.

MEG. What do you mean?

BABE. "Don't make a mess; don't make yourself sick; don't cut yourself with that sharp knife." She's turning into Old Grandmama.

MEG. You think so?

BABE. More and more. Do you know she's taken to wearing Old Grandmama's torn sunhat and her green garden gloves?

MEG. Those old lime green ones?

BABE. Yeah; she works out in the garden wearing the lime green gloves of a dead woman. Imagine wearing those gloves on your hands.

MEG. Poor Lenny. She needs some love in her life. All she does is work out at that brick yard and take care of Old Granddaddy.

22

BABE. Yeah. But she's so shy with men.

MEG. (*Biting into an apple.*) Probably because of that *shrunken* ovary she has.

BABE. (*Slinging ice cubes.*) Yeah, that *deformed* ovary.

MEG. Old Granddaddy's the one who's made her feel self-conconscious about it. It's his fault. The old fool.

BABE. It's so sad.

MEG. God—you know what?

BABE. What?

MEG. I bet Lenny's never even slept with a man. Just think, thirty years old and never even had it once.

BABE. (*Slyly.*) Oh; I don't know. Maybe she's... had it once?

MEG. She has?

BABE. Maybe. I think so.

MEG. When? When?

BABE. Well... maybe I shouldn't say—

MEG. Babe!

BABE. (*Rapidly telling the story.*) All right then; it was after Old Granddaddy went back to the hospital this second time. Lenny was really in a state of deep depression, I could tell that she was. Then one day she calls me up and asks me to come over and to bring along my polaroid camera. Well, when I arrive she's waiting for me out there in the sun parlour wearing her powder blue Sunday dress and this old curled up wig. She confided that she was gonna try sending in her picture to one of those lonely hearts clubs.

MEG. Oh, my God.

BABE. Lonely Hearts of the South. She'd seen their ad in a magazine.

MEG. Jesus.

BABE. Anyway, I take some snapshots and she sends them on in to the club, and about two weeks later she receives in the mail this whole load of pictures of available men, most of 'em fairly odd looking. But of course she doesn't call any of 'em up 'cause she's real shy. But one of 'em, this Charlie Hill from Memphis, Tennessee, he calls her.

MEG. He does?

BABE. Yeah. And time goes on and she says he's real funny

23

on the phone; so they decide to get together to meet.

MEG. Yeah?!

BABE. Well, he drives down here to Hazlehurst 'bout three or four different times and has supper with her, then one weekend she goes up to Memphis to visit him; and I think that is where it happened.

MEG. What makes you think so?

BABE. Well, when I went to pick her up from the bus depot, she ran off the bus and threw her arms around me and started crying and sobbing as though she'd like to never stop. I asked her, I said, "Lenny, what's the matter?" And she said, "I've done it, Babe! Honey, I have done it!"

MEG. (*Whispering.*) And you think she meant that she'd done *it*?

BABE. (*Whispering back, slyly.*) I think so.

MEG. Well, goddamn! (*They laugh with glee.*)

BABE. But she didn't say anything else about it. She just went on to tell me about the boot factory where Charlie worked and what a nice city Memphis was.

MEG. So, what happened to this Charlie?

BABE. Well, he came to Hazlehurst just one more time. Lenny took him over to meet Old Granddaddy at the hospital and after that they broke it off.

MEG. 'Cause of Old Granddaddy?

BABE. Well, she said it was on account of her missing ovary. That Charlie didn't want to marry her on account of it.

MEG. Ah, how mean. How hateful.

BABE. Oh, it was. He seemed like such a nice man, too—kinda chubby with red hair and freckles, always telling these funny jokes.

MEG. Hmmm, that just doesn't seem right. Something about that doesn't seem exactly right. (*Meg paces about the kitchen and comes across the box of candy Lenny got for her birthday.*) Oh, God. "Happy Birthday to Lenny from the Buck Boyles."

BABE. Oh, no! Today's Lenny's birthday!

MEG. That's right.

BABE. I forgot all about it!

MEG. I know. I did too.

BABE. Gosh, we'll have to order up a big cake for her. She always loves to make those wishes on her birthday cake.

MEG. Yeah, let's get her a big cake! A huge one! (*Suddenly noticing the plastic wrapper on the candy box.*) Oh, God, that Chick's so cheap!

BABE. What do you mean?

MEG. This plastic has poinsettias on it!

BABE. (*Running to see.*) Oh, let me see—(*She looks at the package with disgust.*) Boy, oh, boy! I'm calling that bakery and ordering the very largest size cake they have! That Jumbo Deluxe!

MEG. Good!

BABE. Why, I imagine they can make one up to be about—*this* big. (*She demonstrates.*)

MEG. Oh, at least; at least that big. Why, maybe, it'll even be *this* big. (*She makes a very, very, very, large size cake.*)

BABE. You think it could be *that* big?

MEG. Sure!

BABE. (*After a moment, getting the idea.*) Or, or what if it were *this* big? (*She maps out a cake that covers the room.*) What if we get the cake and it's *this* big?!! (*She gulps down a fistful of cake.*) Gulp! Gulp! Gulp! Tasty treat!

MEG. Hmmm—I'll have me some more! Give me some more of that birthday cake! (*Suddenly there is a loud knock at the door.*)

BARNETTE'S VOICE. Hello . . . hello! May I come in?

BABE. (*To Meg, in a whisper, as she takes cover.*) Who's that?

MEG. I don't know.

BARNETTE'S VOICE. (*Still knocking.*) Hello! Hello, Mrs. Botrelle!

BABE. Oh, shoot! It's that lawyer. I don't want to see him.

MEG. Oh, Babe, come on. You've got to see him sometime.

BABE. No, I don't! (*She starts up the stairs.*) Just tell him I died—I'm going upstairs.

MEG. Oh, Babe! Will you come back here!

BABE. (*As she exits.*) You talk to him, please, Meg. Please! I just don't want to see him—

MEG. Babe—Babe! Oh, shit . . . ah, come on in! Door's open!

25

(Barnette Lloyd, 26, enters carrying a briefcase. He is a slender, intelligent young man with an almost fanatical intensity that he subdues by sheer will.)

BARNETTE. How do you do? I'm Barnette Lloyd.

MEG. Pleased to meet you. I'm Meg Magrath, Babe's older sister.

BARNETTE. Yes, I know. You're the singer.

MEG. Well, yes...

BARNETTE. I came to hear you five different times when you were singing at that club in Biloxi. Greeny's I believe was the name of it.

MEG. Yes, Greeny's.

BARNETTE. You were very good. There was something sad and moving about how you sang those songs. It was like you had some sort of vision. Some special sort of vision.

MEG. Well, thank you. You're very kind. Now...about Babe's case—

BARNETTE. Yes?

MEG. We've just got to win it.

BARNETTE. I intend to.

MEG. Of course. But, ah... *(She looks at him.)* Ah, you know, you're very young.

BARNETTE. Yes. I am. I'm young.

MEG. It's just, I'm concerned, Mr. Lloyd—

BARNETTE. Barnette. Please.

MEG. Barnette; that, ah, just maybe we need someone with, well, with more experience. Someone totally familiar with all the ins and outs and the this and thats of the legal dealings and such. As that.

BARNETTE. Ah, you have reservations.

MEG. *(Relieved.)* Reservations. Yes, I have...reservations.

BARNETTE. Well, possibly it would help you to know that I graduated first in my class from Ole Miss Law School. I also spent three different summers taking advanced courses in criminal law at Harvard Law School. I made A's in all the given courses. I was fascinated!

MEG. I'm sure.

BARNETTE. And even now, I've just completed one year working with Jackson's top criminal law firm, Manchester and Wayne. I was invaluable to them. Indispensable. They offered to double my percentage, if I'd stay on; but I refused. I wanted to return to Hazlehurst and open my own office. The reason being, and this is a key point, that I have a personal vendetta to settle with one Zackery F. Botrelle.

MEG. A personal vendetta?

BARNETTE. Yes, ma'am. You are correct. Indeed, I do.

MEG. Hmmm. A personal vendetta...I think I like that. So you have some sort of a personal vendetta to settle with Zackery?

BARNETTE. Precisely. Just between the two of us, I not only intend to keep that sorry S.O.B. from ever being re-elected to the state senate by exposing his shady, criminal dealings; but I also intend to decimate his personal credibility by exposing him as a bully, a brute, and a red-neck thug!

MEG. Well; I can see that you're—fanatical about this.

BARNETTE. Yes; I am. I'm sorry, if I seem outspoken. But, for some reason, I feel I can talk to you...those songs you sang. Excuse me; I feel like a jackass.

MEG. It's all right. Relax. Relax, Barnette. Let me think this out a minute. (*She takes out a cigarette. He lights it for her.*) Now just exactly how do you intend to get Babe off? You know, keep her out of jail.

BARNETTE. It seems to me that we can get her off with a plea of self-defense, or possibly we could go with innocent by reason of temporary insanity. But basically, I intend to prove that Zackery Botrelle brutalized and tormented this poor woman to such an extent that she had no recourse but to defend herself in the only way she knew how!

MEG. I like that!

BARNETTE. Then, of course, I'm hoping this will break the ice and we'll be able to go on to prove that the man's a total criminal, as well as an abusive bully and contemptible slob!

MEG. That sounds good! To me that sounds very good!

BARNETTE. It's just our basic game plan.

MEG. But, now, how are you going to prove all this about Babe being brutalized? We don't want anyone perjured. I mean to commit perjury.

BARNETTE. Perjury? According to my sources, the'll be no need for perjury.

MEG. You mean it's the truth?

BARNETTE. This is a small town, Miss Magrath. The word gets out.

MEG. It's really the truth?

BARNETTE. (*Opening his briefcase.*) Just look at this. It's a photostatic copy of Mrs. Botrelle's medical chart over the past four years. Take a good look at it, if you want your blood to boil!

MEG. (*Looking over the chart.*) What! What! This is maddening. This is madness! Did he do this to her? I'll kill him; I will—I'll fry his blood!! Did he do this?

BARNETTE. (*Alarmed.*) To tell you the truth, I can't say for certain what was accidental and what was not. That's why I need to talk with Mrs. Botrelle. That's why it's very important that I see her!

MEG. (*Her eyes are wild, as she shoves him toward the door.*) Well, look, I've got to see her first. I've got to talk to her first. What I'll do is I'll give you a call. Maybe you can come back over later on—

BARNETTE. Well, then, here's my card—

MEG. Okay. Goodbye.

BARNETTE. 'Bye!

MEG. Oh, wait! Wait! There's one problem with you.

BARNETTE. What?

MEG. What if you get so fanatically obsessed with this vendetta thing that you forget about Babe? You forget about her and sell her down the river just to get at Zackery. What about that?

BARNETTE. I—wouldn't do that.

MEG. You wouldn't?

BARNETTE. No.

MEG. Why not?

BARNETTE. Because, I'm—I'm fond of her.

MEG. What do you mean you're fond of her?

BARNETTE. Well, she . . . she sold me a pound cake at a bazaar once. And I'm fond of her.

MEG. All right; I believe you. Goodbye.

BARNETTE. Goodbye. (*Barnette exits.*)

MEG. Babe! Babe, come down here! Babe! (*Babe comes hurrying down the stairs.*)

BABE. What? What is it? I called about the cake—

MEG. What did Zackery do to you?

BABE. They can't have it for today.

MEG. Did he hurt you? Did he? Did he do that?

BABE. Oh, Meg, please—

MEG. Did he? Goddamnit, Babe—

BABE. Yes, he did.

MEG. Why? Why?

BABE. I don't know! He started hating me, 'cause I couldn't laugh at his jokes. I just started finding it impossible to laugh at his jokes the way I used to. And then the sound of his voice got to where it tired me out awful bad to hear it. I'd fall asleep just listening to him at the dinner table. He'd say, "Hand me some of that gravy!" Or, "This roast beef is too damn bloody." And suddenly I'd be out cold like a light.

MEG. Oh, Babe. Babe, this is very important. I want you to sit down here and tell me what all happened right before you shot Zackery. That's right, just sit down and tell me.

BABE. (*After a pause.*) I told you I can't tell you on account of I'm protecting someone.

MEG. But Babe, you've just got to talk to someone about all this. You just do.

BABE. Why?

MEG. Because it's a human need. To talk about our lives. It's an important human need.

BABE. Oh. Well, I do feel like I want to talk to someone. I do.

MEG. Then talk to me; please.

BABE. (*A decision.*) All right. (*After thinking a minute.*) I don't know where to start.

MEG. Just start at the beginning. Just there at the beginning.

BABE. (*After a moment.*) Well, do you remember Willie Jay? (*Meg shakes her head.*) Cora's youngest boy?

29

MEG. Oh, yeah, that little kid we used to pay a nickel to, to run down to the drugstore and bring us back a cherry Coke.

BABE. Right. Well, Cora irons at my place on Wednesdays now, and she just happened to mention that Willie Jay'd picked up this old stray dog and that he'd gotten real fond of him. But now they couldn't afford to feed him anymore, so she was gonna have to tell Willie Jay to set him loose in the woods.

MEG. (*Trying to be patient.*) Uh huh.

BABE. Well, I said I liked dogs and if he wanted to bring the dog over here, I'd take care of him. You see, I was alone by myself most of the time 'cause the senate was in session, and Zackery was up in Jackson.

MEG. Uh huh. (*Meg reaches for Lenny's box of birthday candy. She takes little nibbles out of each piece, throughout the rest of the scene.*)

BABE. So the next day, Willie Jay brings over this skinny, old dog with these little crossed-eyes. Well, I asked Willie Jay what his name was, and he said they called him Dog. Well, I liked the name; so I thought I'd keep it.

MEG. (*Getting up.*) Uh huh. I'm listening. I'm just gonna get me a glass of cold water; do you want one?

BABE. Okay.

MEG. So you kept the name—Dog.

BABE. Yeah. Anyway, when Willie Jay was leaving he gave Dog a hug and said, "Goodbye, Dog. You're a fine ole dog." Well, I felt something for him, so I told Willie Jay he could come back and visit with Dog any time he wanted, and his face just kinda lit right up.

MEG. (*Offering the candy.*) Candy—

BABE. No thanks. Anyhow, time goes on and Willie Jay keeps coming over and over. And we talk about Dog and how fat he's getting and then, well, you know, things start up.

MEG. No, I don't know. What things start up?

BABE. Well, things start up. Like sex. Like that.

MEG. Babe, wait a minute—Willie Jay's a boy. A small boy, about this tall. He's about this tall!

BABE. No! Oh, no! He's taller now! He's fifteen now. When you knew him he was only about seven or eight.

MEG. But, even so—fifteen. And he's a black boy; a colored

boy; a Negro.

BABE. (*Flustered.*) Well, I realize that, Meg. Why do you think I'm so worried about his getting public exposure? I don't want to ruin his reputation!

MEG. I'm amazed, Babe. I'm really, completely amazed. I didn't even know you were a liberal.

BABE. Well, I'm not! I'm not a liberal! I'm a democratic! I was just lonely! I was so lonely. And he was good. Oh, he was so, so good. I'd never had it that good. We'd always go out into the garage and—

MEG. It's okay. I've got the picture; I've got the picture! Now, let's just get back to the story. To yesterday, when you shot Zackery.

BABE. All right, then. Let's see... Willie Jay was over. And it was after we'd—

MEG. Yeah! Yeah.

BABE. And we were just standing around on the back porch playing with Dog. Well, suddenly, Zackery comes from around the side of the house. And he startled me 'cause he's supposed to be away at the office, and there he is coming from 'round the side of the house. Anyway, he says to Willie Jay, "Hey, boy, what are you doing back here?" And I said, "He's not doing anything. You just go on home, Willie Jay! You just run right on home." Well, before he can move, Zackery comes up and knocks him once right across the face and then shoves him down the porch steps, causing him to skin up his elbow real bad on that hard concrete. Then he says, "Don't you ever come around here again, or I'll have them cut out your gizzard!" Well, Willie Jay starts crying, these tears come streaming down his face, then he gets up real quick and runs away with Dog following off after him. After that, I don't remember much too clearly; let's see... I went on into the living room, and I went right up to the davenport and opened the drawer where we keep the burglar gun... I took it out. Then I—I brought it up to my ear. That's right. I put it right inside my ear. Why, I was gonna shoot off my own head! That's what I was gonna do. Then I heard the back door slamming and suddenly, for some reason, I thought about mama... how she'd hung herself. And here I was about ready to shoot myself. Then I realized—that's right I realized how I didn't want to kill myself! And she—she probably didn't want to kill herself. She wanted to kill him, and I wanted to kill him, too. I wanted to kill Zackery, not myself 'Cause I—I wanted to live! So I waited for him to come on into the living room. Then I held out the gun, and I pulled the trigger. aiming for his heart, but getting him in the stomach. (*After a pause.*) It's funny that I really did that.

MEG. It's a good thing that you did. It's a damn good thing that you did.

BABE. It was.

MEG. Please, Babe, talk to Barnette Lloyd. Just talk to him and see if he can help.

BABE. But how about Willie Jay?

MEG. (*Starting towards the phone.*) Oh, he'll be all right. You just talk to that lawyer like you did to me. (*Looking at the number on the card, she begins dialing.*) See, 'cause he's gonna be on your side.

BABE. No! Stop, Meg, stop! Don't call him up! Please don't call him up! You can't! It's too awful. (*She runs over and jerks the bottom half of the phone away from Meg. Meg stands, holding the receiver.*)

MEG. Babe! (*Babe slams her half of the phone into the refrigerator.*)

BABE. I just can't tell some stranger all about my personal life. I just can't.

MEG. Well, hell, Babe; you're the one who said you wanted to live.

BABE. That's right. I did. (*She takes the phone out of the refrigerator and hands it to Meg.*) Here's the other part of the phone. (*Babe moves to sit at the kitchen table. Meg takes the phone back to the counter. Babe, as she fishes a lemon out of her glass and begins sucking on it.*) Meg.

MEG. What?

BABE. I called the bakery. They're gonna have Lenny's cake ready first thing tomorrow morning. That's the earliest they can get it.

MEG. All right.

BABE. I told them to write on it, "Happy Birthday Lenny—A

Day Late." That sound okay?

MEG. (*At the phone.*) It sounds nice.

BABE. I ordered up the very largest size cake they have. I told them chocolate cake with white icing and red trim. Think she'll like that?

MEG. (*Dialing on the phone.*) Yeah, I'm sure she will. She'll like it.

BABE. I'm hoping.

BLACKOUT

END OF ACT I

ACT II

The lights go up on the kitchen. It is later that evening on the same day. Meg's suitcase has been moved upstairs. Babe's saxophone has been taken out of the case and put together. Babe and Barnette are sitting at the kitchen table. Barnette is writing and re-checking notes with explosive intensity. Babe, who has changed into a casual shift, sits eating a bowl of oatmeal, slowly.

BARNETTE. (*To himself.*) Mmm-huh! Yes! I see, I see! Well, we can work on that! And of course, this is mere conjecture! Difficult, if not impossible, to prove. Ha! Yes. Yes, indeed. Indeed—

BABE. Sure you don't want any oatmeal?

BARNETTE. What? Oh, no. No, thank you. Let's see, ah, where were we?

BABE. I just shot Zackery.

BARNETTE. (*Looking at his notes.*) Right. Correct. You've just pulled the trigger.

BABE. Tell me, do you think Willie Jay can stay out of all this?

BARNETTE. Believe me, it is in our interest to keep him as far out of this as possible.

BABE. Good.

BARNETTE. (*Throughout the following, Barnette stays glued to Babe's every word.*) All right, you've just shot one Zackery Botrelle, as a result of his continual physical and mental abuse—what happens now?

BABE. Well, after I shot him, I put the gun down on the piano bench and then I went out into the kitchen and made up a pitcher of lemonade.

34

BARNETTE. Lemonade?

BABE. Yes, I was dying of thirst. My mouth was just as dry as a bone.

BARNETTE. So in order to quench this raging thirst that was choking you dry and preventing any possibility of you uttering intelligible sounds or phrases, you went out to the kitchen and made up a pitcher of lemonade?

BABE. Right. I made it just the way I like it with lots of sugar and lots of lemon—about ten lemons in all. Then I added two trays of ice and stirred it up with my wooden stirring spoon.

BARNETTE. Than what?

BABE. Then I drank three glasses, one right after the other. They were large glasses, about this tall. Then suddenly, my stomach kind of swoll all up. I guess what caused it was all that sour lemon.

BARNETTE. Could be.

BABE. Then what I did was...I wiped my mouth off with the back of my hand, like this... (She demonstrates.)

BARNETTE. Hmmm.

BABE. I did it to clear off all those little beads of water that had settled there.

BARNETTE. I see.

BABE. Then I called out to Zackery. I said, "Zackery, I've made some lemonade. Can you use a glass?"

BARNETTE. Did he answer? Did you hear an answer?

BABE. No. He didn't answer.

BARNETTE. So, what'd you do?

BABE. I poured him a glass anyway and took it out to him.

BARNETTE. You took it out to the living room?

BABE. I did. And there he was; lying on the rug. He was looking up at me trying to speak words. I said, "What?...Lemonade? ...You don't want it? Would you like a Coke instead?" Then I got the idea, he was telling me to call on the phone for medical help. So I got on the phone and called up the hospital. I gave my name and address and I told them my husband was shot and he was lying on the rug and there was plenty of blood. (Babe pauses a minute, as Barnette works frantically on his notes.) I guess that's gonna look kinda bad.

BARNETTE. What?

BABE. Me fixing that lemonade, before I called the hospital.

BARNETTE. Well, not . . . necessarily.

BABE. I tell you, I think the reason I made up the lemonade, I mean besides the fact that my mouth was bone dry, was that I was afraid to call the authorities. I was afraid. I—I really think I was afraid they would see that I had tried to shoot Zackery, in fact, that I had shot him, and they would accuse me of possible murder and send me away to jail.

BARNETTE. Well, that's understandable.

BABE. I think so. I mean, in fact, that's what did happen. That's what is happening—'cause here I am just about ready to go right off to the Parchment Prison Farm. Yes, here I am just practically on the brink of utter doom. Why, I feel so all alone.

BARNETTE. Now, now, look—Why, there's no reason for you to get yourself so all upset and worried. Please, don't. Please. (*They look at each other for a moment.*) You just keep filling in as much detailed information as you can about those incidents on the medical reports. That's all you need to think about. Don't you worry, Mrs. Botrelle, we're going to have a solid defense.

BABE. Please, don't call me Mrs. Botrelle.

BARNETTE. All right.

BABE. My name's Becky. People in the family call me Babe; but my real name's Becky.

BARNETTE. All right, Becky. (*Barnette and Babe stare at each other for a long moment.*)

BABE. Are you sure you didn't go to Hazlehurst High?

BARNETTE. No, I went away to a boarding school.

BABE. Gosh, you sure do look familiar. You sure do.

BARNETTE. Well, I—I doubt you'll remember, but I did meet you once.

BABE. You did? When?

BARNETTE. At the Christmas bazaar, year before last. You were selling cakes and cookies and . . . candy.

BABE. Oh, yes! You bought the orange pound cake!

BARNETTE. Right.

BABE. Of course, and then we talked for a while. We talked about the Christmas angel.

BARNETTE. You do remember.

BABE. I remember it very well. You were even thinner then than you are now.

BARNETTE. Well, I'm surprised. I'm certainly...surprised. (*The phone begins to ring.*)

BABE. (*As she goes to answer the phone.*) This is quite a coincidence! Don't you think it is? Why, it's almost a fluke. (*She answers the phone.*) Hello...Oh, hello, Lucille...Oh, he is? ...Oh, he does?...Okay. Oh, Lucille, wait! Has Dog come back to the house?...Oh, I see...Okay. Okay. (*After a brief pause.*) Hello, Zackery? How are you doing?...Uh huh... uh huh...oh, I'm sorry...Please, don't scream...uh huh... uh huh...You want what?...No, I can't come up there now ...Well, for one thing, I don't even have the car. Lenny and Meg are up at the hospital right now, visiting with Old Granddaddy . . . What? . . . Oh, really? . . . Oh, really? . . . Well, I've got me a lawyer that's over here right now, and he's building me up a solid defense!...Wait just a minute, I'll see. (*To Barnette.*) He wants to talk to you. He says he's got some blackening evidence that's gonna convict me of attempting to murder him on the first degree!

BARNETTE. (*Disgustedly.*) Oh, bluff! He's bluffing! Here, hand me the phone. (*He takes the phone and becomes suddenly cool and suave.*) Hello, this is Mr. Barnette Lloyd speaking. I'm Mrs. . . . ah, Becky's attorney . . . Why, certainly, Mr. Botrelle, I'd be more than glad to check out any pertinent information that you may have...Fine, then I'll be right on over. Goodbye. (*He hangs up the phone.*)

BABE. What did he say?

BARNETTE. He wants me to come see him at the hospital this evening. Says he's got some sort of evidence. Sounds highly suspect to me.

BABE. Oooh! Didn't you just hate his voice? Doesn't he have the most awful voice! I just hate! I can't bear to hear it!

BARNETTE. Well, now—now, wait. Wait just a minute.

BABE. What?

BARNETTE. I have a solution. From now on I'll handle all communications between you two. You can simply refuse to speak with him.

37

BABE. All right—I will. I'll do that.

BARNETTE. (*Starting to pack his briefcase.*) Well, I'd better get over there and see just what he's got up his sleeve.

BABE. (*After a pause.*) Barnette.

BARNETTE. Yes?

BABE. What's the personal vendetta about? You know, the one you have to settle with Zackery.

BARNETTE. Oh, it's—it's complicated. It's a very complicated matter.

BABE. I see.

BARNETTE. The major thing he did was to ruin my father's life. He took away his job, his home, his health, his respectability. I don't like to talk about it.

BABE. I'm sorry. I just wanted to say—I hope you win it. I hope you win your vendetta.

BARNETTE. Thank you.

BABE. I think it's an important thing that a person could win a life long vendetta.

BARNETTE. Yes. Well, I'd better be going.

BABE. All right. Let me know what happens.

BARNETTE. I will. I'll get back to you right away.

BABE. Thanks.

BARNETTE. Goodbye, Becky.

BABE. Goodbye, Barnette. (*Barnette exits. Babe looks around the room for a moment, then goes over to her white suitcase and opens it up. She takes out her pink hair curlers and a brush. She begins brushing her hair.*) Goodbye, Becky. Goodbye, Barnette. Goodbye, Becky. Oooh. (*Lenny enters. She is fuming. Babe is rolling her hair throughout most of the following scene.*) Lenny, hi!

LENNY. Hi.

BABE. Where's Meg?

LENNY. Oh, she had to go by the store and pick some things up. I don't know what.

BABE. Well, how's Old Granddaddy?

LENNY. (*As she picks up Babe's bowl of oatmeal.*) He's fine Wonderful! Never been better!

BABE. Lenny, what's wrong? What's the matter?

LENNY. It's Meg! I could just wring her neck! I could just wring it!

BABE. Why? Wha'd she do?

LENNY. She lied! She sat in that hospital room and shamelessly lied to Old Granddaddy. She went on and on telling such untrue stories and lies.

BABE. Well, what? What did she say?

LENNY. Well, for one thing she said she was gonna have a RCA record coming out with her picture on the cover, eating pineapples under a palm tree.

BABE. Well, gosh, Lenny, maybe she is! Don't you think she really is?

LENNY. Babe, she sat here this very afternoon and told me how all that she's done this whole year is work as a clerk for a dog food company.

BABE. Oh, shoot. I'm disappointed.

LENNY. And then she goes on to say that she'll be appearing on the "Johnny Carson Show" in two weeks' time. Two weeks' time! Why, Old Granddaddy's got a TV set right in his room. Imagine what a letdown it's gonna be.

BABE. Why, mercy me.

LENNY. (*Slamming the coffeepot on.*) Oh, and she told him the reason she didn't use the money he sent her to come home Christmas was that she was right in the middle of making a huge multi-million-dollar motion picture and was just under too much pressure.

BABE. My word!

LENNY. The movie's coming out this spring. It's called, "Singing in a Shoe Factory." But she only has a small leading role —not a large leading role.

BABE. (*Laughing.*) For heaven's sake—

LENNY. I'm sizzling. Oh, I just can't help it! I'm sizzling!

BABE. Sometimes Meg does such strange things.

LENNY. (*Slowly, as she picks up the opened box of birthday candy.*) Who ate this candy?

BABE. (*Hesitantly.*) Meg.

LENNY. My one birthday present, and look what she does! Why, she's taken one little bite out of each piece and then just put it back in! Ooh! That's just like her! That is just like her!

BABE. Lenny, please—

LENNY. I can't help it! It gets me mad! It gets me upset! Why, Meg's always run wild—she started smoking and drinking when she was fourteen years old, she never made good grades—never made her own bed! But somehow she always seemed to get what she wanted. She's the one who got singing and dancing lessons; and a store-bought dress to wear to her senior prom. Why do you remember how Meg always got to wear twelve jingle bells on her petticoats, while we were only allowed to wear three apiece? Why?! Why should Old Grandmama let her sew twelve golden jingle bells on her petticoats and us only three!!!

BABE. (*Who has heard all this before.*) I don't know!! Maybe she didn't jingle them as much!

LENNY. I can't help it! It gets me mad! I resent it. I do.

BABE. Oh, don't resent Meg. Things have been hard for Meg. After all, she was the one who found Mama.

LENNY. Oh, I know; she's the one who found Mama. But that's always been the excuse.

BABE. But, I tell you, Lenny, after it happened, Meg started doing all sorts of these strange things.

LENNY. She did? Like what?

BABE. Like things I never wanted to tell you about.

LENNY. What sort of things?

BABE. Well, for instance, back when we used to go over to the library, Meg would spend all her time reading and looking through this old, black book called *Diseases of the Skin*. It was full of the most sickening pictures you'd ever seen. Things like rotting-away noses and eyeballs drooping off down the sides of people's faces and scabs and sores and eaten-away places all over *all* parts of people's bodies.

LENNY. (*Trying to pour her coffee.*) Babe, please! That's enough.

BABE. Anyway, she'd spend hours and hours just forcing herself to look through this book. Why, it was the same way she'd force herself to look at the poster of crippled children stuck up in the window at Dixieland Drugs. You know, that one where

40

they want you to give a dime. Meg would stand there and stare at their eyes and look at the braces on their little crippled-up legs — then she'd purposely go and spend her dime on a double scoop ice cream cone and eat it all down. She'd say to me, "See, I can stand it. I can stand it. Just look how I'm gonna be able to stand it."

LENNY. That's awful.

BABE. She said she was afraid of being a weak person. I guess 'cause she cried in bed every night for such a long time.

LENNY. Goodness mercy. (*After a pause.*) Well, I suppose you'd have to be a pretty hard person to be able to do what she did to Doc Porter.

BABE. (*Exasperated.*) Oh, shoot! It wasn't Meg's fault that hurricane wiped Biloxi away. I never understood why people were blaming all that on Meg — just because that roof fell in and crunched Doc's leg. It wasn't her fault.

LENNY. Well, it was Meg who refused to evacuate. Jim Craig and some of Doc's other friends were all down there and they kept trying to get everyone to evacuate. But Meg refused. She wanted to stay on because she thought a hurricane would be — oh, I don't know — a lot of fun. Then everyone says she baited Doc into staying with her. She said she'd marry him if he'd stay.

BABE. (*Taken aback by this new information.*) Well, he has a mind of his own. He could have gone.

LENNY. But he didn't. 'Cause . . . 'cause he loved her. And then after the roof caved, and they got Doc to the high school gym, Meg just left. She just left him there to leave for California — 'cause of her career, she says. I think it was a shameful thing to do. It took almost a year for his leg to heal and after that he gave up his medical career altogether. He said he was tired of hospitals. It's such a sad thing. Everyone always knew he was gonna be a doctor. We've called him Doc for years.

BABE. I don't know. I guess, I don't have any room to talk; 'cause I just don't know. (*Pause.*) Gosh, you look so tired.

LENNY. I feel tired.

BABE. They say women need a lot of iron . . . so they won't feel tired.

LENNY. What's got iron in it? Liver?

41

BABE. Yeah, liver's got it. And vitamin pills. (*After a moment, Meg enters. She carries a bottle of bourbon that is already minus a few slugs and a newspaper. She is wearing black boots, a dark dress, and a hat. The room goes silent.*)

MEG. Hello.

BABE. (*Fooling with her hair.*) Hi, Meg. (*Lenny quietly sips her coffee.*)

MEG. (*Handing the newspaper to Babe.*) Here's your paper.

BABE. Thanks. (*She opens it.*) Oh, here it is, right on the front page. (*Meg lights a cigarette.*) Where's the scissors, Lenny?

LENNY. Look in there in the ribbon drawer.

BABE. Okay. (*Babe gets the scissors and glue out of the drawer and slowly begins cutting out the newspaper article.*)

MEG. (*After a few moments, filled only with the snipping of scissors.*) All right—I lied! I lied! I couldn't help it... these stories just came pouring out of my mouth! When I saw how tired and sick Old Granddaddy'd gotten—they just flew out! All I wanted was to see him smiling and happy. I just wasn't going to sit there and look at him all miserable and sick and sad! I just wasn't!

BABE. Oh, Meg, he is sick, isn't he—

MEG. Why, he's gotten all white and milky—he's almost evaporated!

LENNY. (*Gasping and turning to Meg.*) But still you shouldn't have lied! It just was wrong for you to tell such lies—

MEG. Well, I know that! Don't you think I know that? I hate myself when I lie for that old man. I do. I feel so weak. And then I have to go and do at least three or four things that I know he'd despise just to get even with that miserable, old, bossy man!

LENNY. Oh, Meg, please, don't talk so about Old Granddaddy! It sounds so ungrateful. Why, he went out of his way to make a home for us; to treat us like we were his very own children. All he ever wanted was the best for us. That's all he ever wanted.

MEG. Well, I guess it was; but sometimes I wonder what we wanted.

BABE. (*Taking the newspaper article and glue over to her suit-*

case.) Well, one thing I wanted was a team of white horses to ride Mama's coffin to her grave. That's one thing I wanted. (*Lenny and Meg exchange looks.*) Lenny, did you remember to pack my photo album?

LENNY. It's down there at the bottom, under all that night stuff.

BABE. Oh, I found it.

LENNY. Really, Babe, I don't understand why you have to put in the articles that are about the unhappy things in your life. Why would you want to remember them?

BABE. (*Pasting the article in.*) I don't know. I just like to keep an accurate record, I suppose. There. (*She begins flipping through the book.*) Look, here's a picture of me when I got married.

MEG. Let's see. (*Babe brings the photo album over to the table. They all look at it.*)

LENNY. My word, you look about twelve years old.

BABE. I was just eighteen.

MEG. You're smiling, Babe. Were you happy then?

BABE. (*Laughing.*) Well, I was drunk on champagne punch. I remember that! (*They turn the page.*)

LENNY. Oh, there's Meg singing at Greeny's!

BABE. Oooh, I wish you were still singing at Greeny's! I wish you were!

LENNY. You're so beautiful!

BABE. Yes, you are. You're beautiful.

MEG. Oh, stop! I'm not—

LENNY. Look, Meg's starting to cry.

BABE. Oh, Meg—

MEG. I'm not—

BABE. Quick, better turn the page; we don't want Meg crying— (*She flips the pages.*)

LENNY. Why, it's Daddy.

MEG. Where'd you get that picture, Babe? I thought she burned them all.

BABE. Ah, I just found it around.

LENNY. What does it say here? What's that inscription?

BABE. It says "Jimmy—clowning at the beach—1952."

LENNY. Well, will you look at that smile.

MEG. Jesus, those white teeth—turn the page, will you; we can't do any worse than this! (*They turn the page. The room goes silent.*)

BABE. It's Mama and the cat.

LENNY. Oh, turn the page—

BABE. That old yellow cat. You know, I bet if she hadn't of hung that old cat along with her, she wouldn't have gotten all that national coverage.

MEG. (*After a moment, hopelessly.*) Why are we talking about this?

LENNY. Meg's right. It was so sad. It was awfully sad. I remember how we all three just sat up on that bed the day of the service all dressed up in our black velveteen suits crying the whole morning long.

BABE. We used up one whole big box of Kleenexes.

MEG. And then Old Granddaddy came in and said he was gonna take us out to breakfast. Remember, he told us not to cry anymore 'cause he was gonna take us out to get banana splits for breakfast.

BABE. That's right—banana splits for breakfast!

MEG. Why, Lenny was fourteen years old and he thought that would make it all better—

BABE. Oh, I remember he said for us to eat all we wanted. I think I ate about five! He kept shoving them down us!

MEG. God, we were so sick!

LENNY. Oh, we were!

MEG. (*Laughing.*) Lenny's face turned green—

LENNY. I was just as sick as a dog!

BABE. Old Grandmama was furious!

LENNY. Oh, she was!

MEG. The thing about Old Granddaddy is he keeps trying to make us happy and we end up getting stomach aches and turning green and throwing up in the flower arrangements.

BABE. Oh, that was me! I threw up in the flowers! Oh, no' How embarrassing!

LENNY. (*Laughing.*) Oh, Babe—

BABE. (*Hugging her sisters.*) Oh, Lenny! Oh, Meg!

MEG. Oh, Babe! Oh, Lenny! It's so good to be home!

LENNY. Hey, I have an idea—

BABE. What?

LENNY. Let's play cards!!

BABE. Oh, let's do!

MEG. All right!

LENNY. Oh, good! It'll be just like when we used to sit around the table playing hearts all night long.

BABE. I know! (*Getting up.*) I'll fix us up some popcorn and hot chocolate—

MEG. (*Getting up.*) Here, let me get out that old black popcorn pot.

LENNY. (*Getting up.*) Oh, yes! Now, let's see, I think I have a deck of cards around here somewhere.

BABE. Gosh, I hope I remember all the rules—Are hearts good or bad?

MEG. Bad, I think. Aren't they, Lenny?

LENNY. That's right. Hearts are bad, but the Black Sister is the worst of all—

MEG. Oh, that's right! And the Black Sister is the Queen of Spades.

BABE. (*Figuring it out.*) And spades are the black cards that aren't the puppy dog feet?

MEG. (*Thinking a moment.*) Right. And she counts a lot of points.

BABE. And points are bad?

MEG. Right. Here, I'll get some paper so we can keep score. (*The phone begins to ring.*)

LENNY. Oh, here they are!

MEG. I'll get it—

LENNY. Why, look at these cards! They're years old!

BABE. Oh, let me see!

MEG. Hello...No, this is Meg Magrath...Doc. How are you? ...Well, good...You're where?... Well, sure. Come on over ...Sure, I'm sure. Yeah, come right on over...All right. Bye. (*She hangs up.*) That was Doc Porter. He's down the street at Al's Grill. He's gonna come on over.

LENNY. He is?

MEG. He said he wanted to come see me.

LENNY. Oh. (*After a pause.*) Well, do you still want to play?
MEG. No, I don't think so.
LENNY. All right. (*Lenny starts to shuffle the cards, as Meg brushes her hair.*) You know, it's really not much fun playing Hearts with only two people.
MEG. I'm sorry; maybe after Doc leaves, I'll join you.
LENNY. I know; maybe Doc'll want to play, then we can have a game of bridge.
MEG. I don't think so. Doc never liked cards. Maybe we'll just go out somewhere.
LENNY. (*Putting down the cards. Babe picks them up.*) Meg—
MEG. What?
LENNY. Well, Doc's married now.
MEG. I know. You told me.
LENNY. Oh. Well, as long as you know that. (*Pause.*) As long as you know that.
MEG. (*Still primping.*) Yes, I know. She made the pot.
BABE. How many cards do I deal out?
LENNY. (*Leaving the table.*) Excuse me.
BABE. All of 'em, or what?
LENNY. Ah, Meg? Could I—could I ask you something? (*Babe proceeds to deal out all the cards.*)
MEG. What?
LENNY. I just wanted to ask you—
MEG. What? (*Unable to go on with what she really wants to say, Lenny runs up and picks up the box of candy.*)
LENNY. Well, just why did you take one little bite out of each piece of candy in this box and then just put it back in?
MEG. Oh. Well, I was looking for the ones with nuts.
LENNY. The ones with nuts.
MEG. Yeah.
LENNY. But there are none with nuts. It's a box of assorted cremes—all it has in it are cremes!
MEG. Oh.
LENNY. Why couldn't you just read on the box? It says right here, "Assorted Cremes," not nuts! Besides this was a birthday present to me! My one and only birthday present; my only one!
MEG. I'm sorry. I'll get you another box.

46

LENNY. I don't want another box. That's not the point!

MEG. What is the point?

LENNY. I don't know; it's—it's—You have no respect for other people's property! You just take whatever you want. You just take it! Why, remember how you had layers and layers of jingle bells sewed onto your petticoats while Babe and I only had three apiece?!

MEG. Oh, God! She's starting up about those stupid jingle bells!

LENNY. Well, it's an example! A specific example of how you always got what you wanted!

MEG. Oh, come on, Lenny, you're just upset because Doc called.

LENNY. Who said anything about Doc? Do you think I'm upset about Doc? Why, I've long since given up worrying about you and all your men.

MEG. (*Turning in anger.*) Look, I know I've had too many men. Believe me, I've had way too many men. But it's not my fault you haven't had any—or maybe just that one from Memphis.

LENNY. (*Stopping.*) What one from Memphis?

MEG. (*Slowly.*) The one Babe told me about. From the—club.

LENNY. Babe!!!

BABE. Meg!!!

LENNY. How could you?!! I asked you not to tell anyone! I'm so ashamed! How could you?! Who else have you told? Did you tell anyone else?

BABE. (*Overlapping, to Meg.*) Why'd you have to open your big mouth?!

MEG. (*Overlapping.*) How am I supposed to know? You never said not to tell!

BABE. Can't you use your head just for once?!! (*Then to Lenny.*) No, I never told anyone else. Somehow it just slipped out to Meg. Really, it just flew out of my mouth—

LENNY. What do you two have—wings on your tongues?

BABE. I'm sorry, Lenny. Really sorry.

LENNY. I'll just never, never, never be able to trust you again—

MEG. (*Furiously, coming to Babe's defense.*) Oh, for heaven's sake, Lenny, we were just worried about you! We wanted to find a way to make you happy!

LENNY. Happy! Happy! I'll never be happy!

MEG. Well, not if you keep living your life as Old Granddaddy's nursemaid—

BABE. Meg, shut up!

MEG. I can't help it! I just know that the reason you stopped seeing this man from Memphis was because of Old Granddaddy.

LENNY. What—Babe didn't tell you the rest of the story—

MEG. Oh, she said it was something about your shrunken ovary.

BABE. Meg!!

LENNY. Babe!!

BABE. I just mentioned it!

MEG. But I don't believe a word of that story!

LENNY. Oh, I don't care what you believe! It's so easy for you—you always have men falling in love with you! But I have this underdeveloped ovary and I can't have children and my hair is falling out in the comb—so what man can love me?! What man's gonna love me?

MEG. A lot of men!

BABE. Yeah, a lot! A whole lot!

MEG. Old Granddaddy's the only one who seems to think otherwise.

LENNY. 'Cause he doesn't want to see me hurt! He doesn't want to see me rejected and humiliated.

MEG. Oh, come on now, Lenny, don't be so pathetic! God, you make me angry when you just stand there looking so pathetic! Just tell me, did you really ask the man from Memphis? Did you actually ask that man from Memphis all about it?

LENNY. (*Breaking apart.*) No; I didn't. I didn't. Because I just didn't want him not to want me—

MEG. Lenny—

LENNY. (*Furious.*) Don't talk to me anymore! Don't talk to me! I think I'm gonna vomit—I just hope all this doesn't cause me to vomit! (*Lenny exits up the stairs sobbing.*)

MEG. See! See! She didn't even ask him about her stupid ovary! She just broke it all off 'cause of Old Granddaddy! What a jackass fool!

BABE. Oh, Meg, shut up! Why do you have to make Lenny cry? I just hate it when you make Lenny cry! (*Babe runs up the stairs.*) Lenny! Oh, Lenny—(*Meg takes a long sigh and goes to get a cigarette and a drink.*)

MEG. I feel like hell. (*Meg sits in despair—smoking and drinking bourbon. There is a knock at the back door. Meg starts. She brushes her hair out of her face and goes to answer the door. It is Doc.*)

DOC. Hello, Meggy.

MEG. Well, Doc. Well, it's Doc.

DOC. (*After a pause.*) You're home, Meggy.

MEG. Yeah; I've come home. I've come on home to see about Babe.

DOC. And how's Babe?

MEG. Oh, fine. Well, fair. She's fair. (*Doc nods.*) Hey, do you want a drink?

DOC. Whatcha got?

MEG. Bourbon.

DOC. Oh, don't tell me Lenny's stocking bourbon.

MEG. Well, no. I've been to the store. (*Meg gets him a glass and pours them each a drink. They click glasses.*) So, how's your wife?

DOC. She's fine.

MEG. I hear ya got two kids.

DOC. Yeah. Yeah, I got two kids.

MEG. A boy and a girl.

DOC. That's right, Meggy, a boy and a girl.

MEG. That's what you always said you wanted, wasn't it? A boy and a girl.

DOC. Is that what I said?

MEG. I don't know. I thought it's what you said. (*They finish their drinks in silence.*)

DOC. Whose cot?

MEG. Lenny's. She's taken to sleeping in the kitchen.

DOC. Ah. Where is Lenny?

MEG. She's in the upstairs room. I made her cry. Babe's up there seeing to her.

DOC. How'd you make her cry?

MEG. I don't know. Eating her birthday candy; talking on about her boyfriend from Memphis. I don't know. I'm upset about it. She's got a lot on her. Why can't I keep my mouth shut?

DOC. I don't know, Meggy. Maybe it's because you don't want to.

MEG. Maybe. (*They smile at each other. Meg pours each of them another drink.*)

DOC. Well, it's been a long time.

MEG. It has been a long time.

DOC. Let's see—when was the last time we saw each other?

MEG. I can't quite recall.

DOC. Wasn't it in Biloxi?

MEG. Ah, Biloxi. I believe so.

DOC. And wasn't there a—a hurricane going on at the time?

MEG. Was there?

DOC. Yes, there was, one hell of a hurricane. Camille, I believe they called it. Hurricane Camille.

MEG. Yes, now I remember. It was a beautiful hurricane.

DOC. We had a time down there. We had quite a time. Drinking vodka, eating oysters on the half shell, dancing all night long. And the wind was blowing.

MEG. Oh, God, was it blowing.

DOC. Goddamn, was it blowing.

MEG. There never has been such a wind blowing.

DOC. Oh, God, Meggy. Oh, God.

MEG. I know, Doc. It was my fault to leave you. I was crazy. I thought I was choking. I felt choked!

DOC. I felt like a fool.

MEG. No.

DOC. I just kept on wondering why.

MEG. I don't know why... 'Cause I didn't want to care. I don't know. I did care though. I did.

DOC. (*After a pause.*) Ah, hell—(*He pours them both another drink.*) Are you still singing those sad songs?

MEG. No.

DOC. Why not?

MEG. I don't know, Doc. Things got worse for me. After a while, I just couldn't sing anymore. I tell you, I had one hell of a time over Christmas.

DOC. What do you mean?

MEG. I went nuts. I went insane. Ended up in L.A. County Hospital. Psychiatric ward.

DOC. Hell. Ah, hell, Meggy. What happened?

MEG. I don't really know. I couldn't sing anymore; so I lost my job. And I had a bad toothache. I has this incredibly painful toothache. For days I had it, but I wouldn't do anything about it. I just stayed inside my apartment. All I could do was sit around in chairs, chewing on my fingers. Then one afternoon I ran screaming out of the apartment with all my money and jewelry and valuables and tried to stuff it all into one of those March of Dimes collection boxes. That was when they nabbed me. Sad story. Meg goes mad. (*Doc stares at her for a long moment. He pours them both another drink.*)

DOC. (*After quite a pause.*) There's a moon out.

MEG. Is there?

DOC. Wanna go take a ride in my truck and look out at the moon?

MEG. I don't know, Doc. I don't wanna start up. It'll be too hard, if we start up.

DOC. Who says we're gonna start up? We're just gonna look at the moon. For one night just you and me are gonna go for a ride in the country and look out at the moon.

MEG. One night?

DOC. Right.

MEG. Look out at the moon?

DOC. You got it.

MEG. Well . . . all right. (*She gets up.*)

DOC. Better take your coat. (*He helps her into her coat.*) And the bottle—(*He takes the bottle. Meg picks up the glasses.*) Forget the glasses—

MEG. (*Laughing.*) Yeah—forget the glasses. Forget the goddamn glasses. (*Meg shuts off the kitchen lights, leaving the kitchen lit by only a dim light over the kitchen sink. Meg and Doc leave. After a moment, Babe comes down the stairs in her slip.*)

BABE. Meg—Meg? (*She stands for a moment in the moonlight wearing only a slip. She sees her saxophone then moves to pick it up. She plays a few shrieking notes. There is a loud knock on the back door.*)

BARNETTE'S VOICE. Becky! Becky, is that you? (*Babe puts down the saxophone.*)

BABE. Just a minute. I'm coming. (*She puts a raincoat on over her slip and goes to answer the door. It is Barnette.*) Hello, Barnette. Come on in. (*Barnette comes in. He is troubled but is making a great effort to hide the fact.*)

BARNETTE. Thank you.

BABE. What is it?

BARNETTE. I've, ah, I've just come from seeing Zackery at the hospital.

BABE. Oh?

BARNETTE. It seems... Well, it seems his sister, Lucille, was somewhat suspicious.

BABE. Suspicious?

BARNETTE. About you?

BABE. Me?

BARNETTE. She hired a private detective, he took these pictures. (*He hands Babe a small envelope containing several photographs. Babe opens the envelope and begins looking at the pictures in stunned silence.*) They were taken about two weeks ago. It seems, she wasn't going to show them to Botrelle straight away. She, ah, wanted to wait till the time was right. (*The phone rings one and a half times. Barnette glances uneasily towards the phone.*) Becky? (*The phone stops ringing.*)

BABE. (*Looking up at Barnette, slowly.*) These are pictures of Willie Jay and me... out in the garage.

BARNETTE. (*Looking away.*) I know.

BABE. You looked at these pictures?

BARNETTE. Yes—I—well... professionally, I looked at them.

BABE. Oh, mercy. Oh, mercy! We can burn them, can't we? Quick, we can burn them—

BARNETTE. It won't do any good. They have the negatives.

BABE. (*Holding the pictures, as she bangs herself hopelessly into the stove, table, cabinets, etc.*) Oh, no; oh, no; oh, no! Oh, no—

BARNETTE. There—there, now—there—

LENNY'S VOICE. Babe? Are you all right? Babe—

BABE. (*Hiding the pictures.*) What? I'm all right. Go on back to bed. (*Lenny comes down the stairs. She is wearing a coat and wiping white night cream off of her face with a wash rag.*)

LENNY. What's the matter? What's going on down here?

BABE. Nothin! (*Then as she begins dancing ballet style around the room.*) We're—we're just dancing. We were just dancing around down here. (*Signaling to Barnette to dance.*)

LENNY. Well, you'd better get your shoes on, 'cause we've got—

BABE. All right, I will! That's a good idea! (*As she goes to get her shoes, she hides the pictures.*) Now, you go on back to bed. It's pretty late and—

LENNY. Babe, will you listen a minute—

BABE. (*Holding up her shoes.*) I'm putting 'em on—

LENNY. That was the hospital that just called. We've got to get over there. Old Granddaddy's had himself another stroke.

BABE. Oh. All right. My shoes are on. (*She stands. They all look at each other as the lights blackout.*)

END OF ACT II

ACT III

The lights go up on the empty kitchen. It is the following morning. After a few moments, Babe enters from the back door. She is carrying her hair curlers in her hands. She goes and lies down on the cot. A few moments later, Lenny enters. She is tired and weary. Chick's voice is heard.

CHICK'S VOICE. Lenny! Oh, Lenny! (*Lenny turns to the door. Chick enters energetically.*) Well...how is he?

LENNY. He's stabilized; they say for now his functions are all stabilized.

CHICK. Well, is he still in the coma?

LENNY. Uh huh.

CHICK. Hmmm. So do they think he's gonna be...passing on?

LENNY. He may be. He doesn't look so good. They said they'd phone us if there were any sudden changes.

CHICK. Well, it seems to me we'd better get busy phoning on the phone ourselves. (*Removing a list from her pocket.*) Now I've made out this list of all the people we need to notify about Old Granddaddy's predicament. I'll phone half if you'll phone half.

LENNY. But—what would we say?

CHICK. Just tell them the facts; that Old Granddaddy's got himself in a coma, and it could be, he doesn't have long for this world.

LENNY. I—I don't know. I don't feel like phoning.

CHICK. Why, Lenora, I'm surprised, how can you be this way? I went to all the trouble of making up the list. And I offered to phone half of the people on it, even though I'm only one-fourth of the granddaughters. I mean, I just get tired of doing more than my fair share, when people like Meg can suddenly just disappear to where they can't even be reached in case of emergency!

LENNY. All right; give me the list. I'll phone half.

CHICK. Well, don't do it just to suit me.

LENNY. (*She wearily tears the list into two halves.*) I'll phone these here.

CHICK. (*Taking her half of the list.*) Fine then. Suit yourself. Oh, wait—let me call Sally Bell. I need to talk to her anyway.

LENNY. All right.

CHICK. So you add Great Uncle Spark Dude to your list.

LENNY. Okay.

CHICK. Fine. Well, I've got to get on back home and see to the kids. It is gonna be an uphill struggle till I can find someone to replace that good-for-nothing Annie May Jenkins. Well, you let me know if you hear anymore.

LENNY. All right.

CHICK. Goodbye, Rebecca. I said goodbye. (*Babe blows her sax. Chick starts to exit in a flurry then pauses to add:*) And you really ought to try to get that phoning done before twelve noon. (*Chick exits.*)

LENNY. (*After a long pause.*) Babe; I feel bad. I feel real bad.

BABE. Why, Lenny?

LENNY. Because yesterday I—I wished it.

BABE. You wished what?

LENNY. I wished that Old Granddaddy would be put out of his pain. I wished on one of my birthday candles. I did. And now he's in this coma, and they say he's feeling no pain.

BABE. Well, when did you have a cake yesterday? I don't remember you having any cake.

LENNY. Well, I didn't...have a cake. But I just blew out the candles anyway.

BABE. Oh. Well, those birthday wishes don't count unless you have a cake.

LENNY. They don't?

BABE. No. A lot of times they don't even count when you do have a cake. It just depends.

LENNY. Depends on what?

BABE. On how deep your wish is, I suppose.

LENNY. Still, I just wish I hadn't of wished it. Gosh, I wonder when Meg's coming home.

BABE. Should be soon.

LENNY. I just wish we wouldn't fight all the time. I don't like it when we do.

BABE. Me, neither.

LENNY. I guess it hurts my feelings, a little, the way Old Grand-daddy's always put so much stock in Meg and all her singing talent. I think I've been, well, envious of her 'cause I can't seem to do too much.

BABE. Why, sure you can.

LENNY. I can?

BABE. Sure. You just have to put your mind to it; that's all. It's like how I went out and bought that saxophone, just hoping I'd be able to attend music school and start up my own career. I just went out and did it. Just on hope. Of course, now it looks like... Well, it just doesn't look like things are gonna work out for me. But I know they would for you.

LENNY. Well, they'll work out for you, too.

BABE. I doubt it.

LENNY. Listen, I heard up at the hospital that Zackery's already in fair condition. They say soon he'll probably be able to walk and everything.

BABE. Yeah. And life sure can be miserable.

LENNY. Well, I know, 'cause—day before yesterday, Billy Boy was struck down by lightning.

BABE. He was?

LENNY. (*Nearing sobs.*) Yeah. He was struck dead.

BABE. (*Crushed.*) Life sure can be miserable. (*They sit together for several moments in morbid silence. Meg is heard singing a loud happy song. She suddenly enters through the dining room door. She is exuberant! Her hair is a mess and the heel of one shoe has broken off. She is laughing radiantly and limping as*

56

she sings into the broken heel.)

MEG. (*Spotting her sisters.*) Good morning! Good morning! Oh, it's a wonderful morning! I tell you, I am surprised I feel this good. I should feel like hell. By all accounts, I should feel like utter hell! (*She is looking for the glue.*) Where's that glue? This damn heel has broken off my shoe. La, la, la, la, la! Ah, here it is! Now let me just get these shoes off. Zip, zip, zip, zip, zip! Well, what's wrong with you two? My God, you look like doom! (*Babe and Lenny stare helplessly at Meg.*) Oh, I know, you're mad at me 'cause I stayed out all night long. Well; I did.

LENNY. No, we're—we're not mad at you. We're just...depressed. (*She starts to sob.*)

MEG. Oh, Lenny, listen to me, now, everything's all right with Doc. I mean nothing happened. Well, actually a lot did happen, but it didn't come to anything. Not because of me, I'm afraid. (*Smearing glue on her heel.*) I mean, I was out there thinking, "What will I say when he begs me to run away with him? Will I have pity on his wife and those two half-Yankee children? I mean, can I sacrifice their happiness for mine? Yes! Oh, yes! Yes, I can!" But... he didn't ask me. He didn't even want to ask me. I could tell by this certain look in his eyes that he didn't even want to ask me. Why aren't I miserable! Why aren't I morbid! I should be humiliated! Devastated! Maybe these feelings are coming—I don't know. But for now it was...just such fun. I'm happy. I realized I could care about someone. I could want someone. And I sang! I sang all night long! I sang right up into the trees! But not for Old Granddaddy. None of it was to please Old Granddaddy! (*Lenny and Babe look at each other.*)

BABE. Ah, Meg—

MEG. What—

BABE. Well, it's just—It's...

LENNY. It's about Old Granddaddy—

MEG. Oh, I know; I know. I told him all those stupid lies. Well, I'm gonna go right over there this morning and tell him the truth. I mean every horrible thing. I don't care if he wants to

hear it or not. He's just gonna have to take me like I am. And
if he can't take it, if it sends him into a coma, that's just too
damn bad! (*Babe and Lenny look at each other Babe cracks
a smile. Lenny cracks a smile.*)

BABE. You're too late—Ha, ha, ha! (*They both break up laughing.*)

LENNY. Oh, stop! Please! Ha, ha, ha!

MEG. What is it? What's so funny?

BABE. (*Still laughing.*) It's not—It's not funny!

LENNY. (*Still laughing.*) No, it's not! It's not a bit funny!

MEG. Well, what is it then? What?

BABE. (*Trying to calm down.*) Well, it's just—it's just—

MEG. What?

BABE. Well, Old Granddaddy—he—he's in a coma! (*Babe and
Lenny break up laughing.*)

MEG. He's what?

BABE. (*Shrieking.*) In a coma!

MEG. My God! That's not funny!

BABE. (*Calming down.*) I know. I know. For some reason it
just struck us as funny.

LENNY. I'm sorry. It's—it's not funny. It's sad. It's very sad.
We've been up all night long.

BABE. We're really tired.

MEG. Well, my God. How is he? Is he gonna live? (*Babe and
Lenny look at each other.*)

BABE. They don't think so! (*They both break up again.*)

LENNY. Oh, I don't know why we're laughing like this. We're
just sick! We're just awful!

BABE. We are—we're awful!

LENNY. (*As she collects herself.*) Oh, good; now I feel bad.
Now, I feel like crying. I do; I feel like crying.

BABE. Me, too. Me, too.

MEG. Well, you've gotten me depressed!

LENNY. I'm sorry. I'm sorry. It, ah happened last night. He
had another stroke. (*They laugh again.*)

MEG. I see.

LENNY. But he's stabilized now. (*She chokes up once more.*)

MEG. That's good. You two okay? (*Babe and Lenny nod.*) You look like you need some rest. (*Babe and Lenny nod again. Meg goes on, about her heel.*) I hope that'll stay. (*Meg puts the top on the glue. A realization—*) Oh, of course, now I won't be able to tell him the truth about all those lies I told. I mean, finally, I get my wits about me, and he conks out. It's just like him. Babe, can I wear your slippers till this glue dries?

BABE. Sure.

LENNY. (*After a pause.*) Things sure are gonna be different around here ... when Old Granddaddy dies. Well, not for you two really, but for me.

MEG. It'll work out.

BABE. (*Depressed.*) Yeah. It'll work out.

LENNY. I hope so. I'm afraid of being here all by myself. All alone.

MEG. Well, you don't have to be alone. Maybe Babe'll move back in here. (*Lenny looks at Babe hopefully.*)

BABE. No; I don't think I'll be living here.

MEG. (*Realizing her mistake.*) Well, anyway, you're your own woman. Invite some people over. Have some parties. Go out with strange men.

LENNY. I don't know any strange men.

MEG. Well you know that Charlie.

LENNY. (*Shaking her head.*) Not anymore.

MEG. Why not?

LENNY. (*Breaking down.*) I told him we should never see each other again.

MEG. Well; if you told him, you can just untell him.

LENNY. Oh, no I couldn't. I'd feel like a fool.

MEG. Oh, that's not a good enough reason! All people in love feel like fools. Don't they, Babe?

BABE. Sure.

MEG. Look, why don't you give him a call right now? See how things stand?

LENNY. Oh, no! I'd be too scared—

MEG. But what harm could it possibly do? I mean, it's not gonna make things any worse than this never seeing him again, at all, forever.

LENNY. I suppose that's true—

MEG. Of course it is; so call him up! Take a chance, will you? Just take some sort of chance!

LENNY. You think I should?

MEG. Of course! You've got to try—You do! (*Lenny looks over at Babe.*)

BABE. You do, Lenny—I think you do.

LENNY. Really? Really, really?

MEG. Yes! Yes!

BABE. You should!

LENNY. All right. I will! I will!

MEG. Oh, good!

BABE. Good!

LENNY. I'll call him right now, while I've got my confidence up!

MEG. Have you got the number?

LENNY. Uh huh. But, ah, I think I wanna call him upstairs. It'll be more private.

MEG. Ah, good idea.

LENNY. I'm just gonna go on; and call him up; and see what happens—(*She has started up the stairs.*) Wish me good luck!

MEG. Good luck!

BABE. Good luck, Lenny!

LENNY. Thanks. (*Lenny gets almost out of sight, when the phone begins to ring. She stops, Meg picks up the phone.*)

MEG. Hello? (*Then in a whisper.*) Oh, thank you very much ... Yes, I will. 'Bye, 'bye.

LENNY. Who was it?

MEG. Wrong number. They wanted Weed's Body Shop.

LENNY. Oh. Well, I'll be right back down in a minute. (*Lenny exits.*)

MEG. (*After a moment, whispering to Babe.*) That was the bakery; Lenny's cake is ready!

BABE. (*Who has become increasingly depressed.*) Oh.

MEG. I think I'll sneak on down to the corner and pick it up. (*She starts to leave.*)

BABE. Meg—

MEG. What?

BABE. Nothing.

MEG. You okay? (*Babe shakes her head.*) What is it?

BABE. It's just—

MEG. What? (*Babe gets up and goes to her suitcase. She opens it and removes the envelope containing the photographs.*)

BABE. Here. Take a look.

MEG. (*Taking the envelope.*) What is it?

BABE. It's some evidence Zackery's collected against me. Looks like my goose is cooked. (*Meg opens the envelope and looks at the photographs.*)

MEG. My God, it's—it's you and . . . is *that* Willie Jay?

BABE. Yeh.

MEG. Well, he certainly *has* grown. You were right about that. My, oh, my.

BABE. Please don't tell Lenny. She'd hate me.

MEG. I won't. I won't tell Lenny. (*Putting the pictures back into the envelope.*) What are you gonna do?

BABE. What can I do? (*There is a knock on the door. Babe grabs the envelope and hides it.*)

MEG. Who is it?

BARNETTE'S VOICE. It's Barnette Lloyd.

MEG. Oh. Come on in, Barnette. (*Barnette enters. His eyes are ablaze with excitement.*)

BARNETTE. (*As he paces around the room.*) Well; good morning! (*Shaking Meg's hand.*) Good morning, Miss Magrath. (*Touching Babe on the shoulder.*) Becky. (*Moving away.*) What I meant to say is . . . how are you doing this morning?

MEG. Ah—fine. Fine.

BARNETTE. Good. Good. I—I just had time to drop by for a minute.

MEG. Oh.

BARNETTE. So, ah, how's your Granddad doing?

MEG. Well, not very, ah—ah, he's in this coma. (*She breaks up laughing.*)

BARNETTE. I see...I see. (*To Babe.*) Actually, the primary reason I came by was to pick up that—envelope. I left it here last night in all the confusion. (*Pause.*) You, ah, still do have it? (*Babe hands him the envelope.*) Yes. (*Taking the envelope.*) That's the one. I'm sure it'll be much better off in my office safe. (*He puts the envelope into his coat pocket.*)

MEG. I'm sure it will.

BARNETTE. Beg your pardon?

BABE. It's all right. I showed her the pictures.

BARNETTE. Ah; I see.

MEG. So what's going to happen now, Barnette? What are those pictures gonna mean?

BARNETTE. (*After pacing a moment.*) Hmmm. May I speak frankly and openly?

BABE. Uh huh.

MEG. Please do—

BARNETTE. Well, I tell you now, at first glance, I admit those pictures had me considerably perturbed and upset. Perturbed to the point that I spent most of last night going over certain suspect papers and reports that had fallen into my hands—rather recklessly.

BABE. What papers do you mean?

BARNETTE. Papers that pending word from three varied and unbiased experts, could prove graft, fraud, forgery, as well as a history of unethical behavior.

MEG. You mean about Zackery?

BARNETTE. Exactly. You see, I now intend to make this matter just as sticky and gritty for one Z. Botrelle as it is for us. Why, with the amount of scandal I'll dig up, Botrelle will be forced to settle this affair on our own terms!

MEG. Oh, Babe! Did you hear that?!

BABE. Yes! Oh, yes! So you've won it! You've won your lifelong vendetta!

BARNETTE. Well...well, now of course it's problematic in

that, well, in that we won't be able to expose him openly in the courts. That was the original game plan.

BABE. But why not? Why?

BARNETTE. Well, it's only that if, well, if a jury were to—to get, say, a glance at these, ah, photographs, well...well possibly...

BABE. We could be sunk.

BARNETTE. In a sense. But! On the other hand, if a newspaper were to get a hold of our little item, Mr. Zackery Botrelle could find himself boiling in some awfully hot water. So what I'm looking for very simply, is—a deal.

BABE. A deal?

MEG. Thank you, Barnette. It's a sunny day, Babe. (*Realizing she is in the way.*) Ooh, where's that broken shoe? (*She grabs her boots and runs upstairs.*)

BABE. So, you're having to give up your vendetta?

BARNETTE. Well, in a way. For the time. It, ah, seems to me you shouldn't always let your life be ruled by such things as, ah, personal vendettas. (*Looking at Babe with meaning.*) Other things can be important.

BABE. I don't know, I don't exactly know. How 'bout Willie Jay? Will he be all right?

BARNETTE. Yes, it's all been taken care of. He'll be leaving incognito on the midnight bus—heading north.

BABE. North.

BARNETTE. I'm sorry, it seemed the only...way. (*Barnette moves to her—She moves away.*)

BABE. Look, you'd better be getting on back to your work.

BARNETTE. (*Awkwardly.*) Right—'cause I—I've got those important calls out. (*Full of hope for her.*) They'll be pouring in directly. (*He starts to leave, then says to her with love.*) We'll talk.

MEG. (*Reappearing in her boots.*) Oh, Barnette—

BARNETTE. Yes?

MEG. Could you give me a ride just down to the corner? I need to stop at Helen's Bakery.

BARNETTE. Be glad to.

MEG. Thanks. Listen, Babe, I'll be right back with the cake. We're gonna have the best celebration! Now, ah, if Lenny asks where I've gone, just say I'm . . . just say, I've gone out back to, ah, pick up some paw paws! Okay?

BABE. Okay.

MEG. Fine; I'll be back in a bit. Goodbye.

BABE. 'Bye.

BARNETTE. Goodbye, Becky.

BABE. Goodbye, Barnette. Take care. (*Meg and Barnette exit. Babe sits staring ahead, in a state of deep despair.*) Goodbye, Becky. Goodbye, Barnette. Goodbye, Becky. (*She stops when Lenny comes down the stairs in a fluster.*)

LENNY. Oh! Oh! Oh! I'm so ashamed! I'm such a coward! I'm such a yellow-bellied chicken! I'm so ashamed! Where's Meg?

BABE. (*Suddenly bright.*) She's, ah—gone out back—to pick up some paw paws.

LENNY. Oh. Well, at least I don't have to face her! I just couldn't do it! I couldn't make the call!! My heart was pounding like a hammer. Pound! Pound! Pound! Why, I looked down and I could actually see my blouse moving back and forth! Oh, Babe, you look so disappointed. Are you?

BABE. (*Despondently.*) Uh huh.

LENNY. Oh, no! I've disappointed Babe! I can't stand it! I've gone and disappointed my little sister, Babe! Oh, no! I feel like howling like a dog!

CHICK'S VOICE. Oooh, Lenny! (*Chick enters dramatically; dripping with sympathy.*) Well, I just don't know what to say! I'm so sorry! I am so sorry for you! And for Little Babe, here, too. I mean to have such a sister as that!

LENNY. What do you mean?

CHICK. Oh, you don't need to pretend with me. I saw it al! from over there in my own backyard; I saw Meg stumbling out of Doc Porter's pickup truck, not 15 minutes ago. And her looking such a disgusting mess. You must be so ashamed! You must just want to die! Why, I always said that girl was nothing but cheap Christmas trash!

LENNY. Don't talk that way about Meg.

CHICK. Oh, come on now. Lenny, honey, I know exactly how you feel about Meg. Why, Meg's a low-class tramp and you need not have one more blessed thing to do with her and her disgusting behavior.

LENNY. I said don't you ever talk that way about my sister Meg again.

CHICK. Well, my goodness gracious, Lenora, don't be such a noodle—it's the truth!

LENNY. I don't care if it's the Ten Commandments. I don't want to hear it in my home. Not ever again.

CHICK. In your home?! Why, I never in all my life—This is my Grandfather's home! And you're just living here on his charity; so don't you get high-falutin' with me, Miss Lenora Josephine Magrath!

LENNY. Get out of here—

CHICK. Don't you tell me to get out! What makes you think you can order me around? Why, I've had just about my fill of you trashy Magraths and your trashy ways; hanging your selves in cellars; carrying on with married men; shooting your own husbands!

LENNY. Get out!

CHICK. (*To Babe.*) And don't think she's not gonna end up at the state prison farm or in some—mental institution. Why it's a clear-cut case of manslaughter with intent to kill!

LENNY. Out! Get out!

CHICK. (*Running on.*) That's what everyone's saying, deliberate intent to kill! And you'll pay for that! Do you hear me? You'll pay!

LENNY. (*She picks up a broom and threatens Chick with it.*) And I'm telling you to get out!

CHICK. You—you put that down this minute—are you a raving lunatic?

LENNY. (*Beating Chick with the broom.*) I said for you to get out! That means out! And never, never, never come back!

CHICK. (*Overlapping, as she runs around the room.*) Oh! Oh!

Oh! You're crazy! You're crazy!

LENNY. (*Chasing Chick out the door.*) Do you hear me, Chick the Stick! This is my home! This is my house! Get out! Out!

CHICK. (*Overlapping.*) Oh! Oh! Police! Police! You're crazy! Help! Help! (*Lenny chases Chick out of the house. They are both screaming. The phone rings. Babe goes and picks it up.*)

BABE. Hello?...Oh, hello, Zackery!...Yes, he showed them to me!...You're what!...What do you mean?...What!... You can't put me out to Whitfield...'Cause I'm not crazy... I'm not! I'm not!...She wasn't crazy either...Don't you call my mother crazy!...No, you're not! You're not gonna. You're not! (*She slams the phone down and stares wildly ahead.*) He's not. He's not. (*As she walks over to the ribbon drawer.*) I'll do it. I will. And he won't...(*She opens the drawer; pulls out the rope; becomes terrified; throws the rope back in the drawer and slams it shut. Lenny enters from the back door swinging the broom and laughing.*)

LENNY. Oh, my! Oh, my! You should have seen us! Why, I chased Chick the Stick right up the mimosa tree. I did! I left her right up there screaming in the tree!

BABE. (*Laughing; she is insanely delighted.*) Oh, you did!

LENNY. Yes, I did! And I feel so good! I do! I feel good! I feel good!

BABE. (*Overlapping.*) Good! Good, Lenny! Good for you! (*They dance around the kitchen.*)

LENNY. (*Stopping.*) You know what—

BABE. What?

LENNY. I'm gonna call Charlie!!! I'm gonna call him right now!

BABE. You are?

LENNY. Yeah, I feel like I can really do it!

BABE. You do?

LENNY. My courage is up; my heart's in it; the time is right! No more beating around the bush! Let's strike while the iron is hot!

BABE. Right! Right! No more beating around the bush! Strike while the iron is not! (*Lenny goes to the phone. Babe rushes over to the ribbon drawer. She begins tearing through it.*)

LENNY. (*With the receiver in her hand.*) I'm calling him up, Babe—I'm really gonna do it!

BABE. (*Still tearing through the drawer.*) Good! Do it! Good!

LENNY. (*As she dials.*) Look. My hands aren't even shaking.

BABE. (*Pulling out a red cord of rope.*) Don't we have any stronger rope than this?

LENNY. I guess not. All the rope we've got's in that drawer. (*About her hands.*) Now they're shaking a little. (*Babe takes the rope and goes up the stairs. Lenny finishes dialing the number. She waits for an answer.*) Hello?...Hello, Charlie. This is Lenny Magrath...Well, I'm fine. I'm just fine. (*An awkward pause.*) I was, ah, just calling to see—how you're getting on...Well, good. Good...Yes, I know I said that. Now I wish I didn't say it...Well, the reason I said that before, about not seeing each other again, was 'cause of me, not you...Well, it's just I—can't have any children. I—have this ovary problem...Why, Charlie, what a thing to say!...Well, they're not all little snot-nosed pigs!...You think they are!...Oh, Charlie, stop, stop! You're making me laugh...Yes, I guess I was. I can see now that I was...You are?...Well, I'm dying to see you, too... Well, I don't know when, Charlie...soon. How about, well, how about tonight? . . . You will? . . . Oh, you will! . . . All right, I'll be here. I'll be right here...Goodbye, then, Charlie. Goodbye for now. (*She hangs up the phone in a daze.*) Babe. Oh, Babe! He's coming. He's coming! Babe! Oh, Babe, where are you? Meg! Oh...out back—picking up paw paws.(*As she exits through the back door.*) And those paw paws are just ripe for picking up! (*There is a moment of silence, then a loud, horrible thud is heard coming from upstairs. The telephone begins ringing immediately. It rings five times before Babe comes hurrying down the stairs with a broken piece of rope hanging around her neck. The phone continues to ring.*)

BABE. (*To the phone.*) Will you shut up! (*She is jerking the rope from around her neck. She grabs a knife to cut it off.*) Cheap! Miserable! I hate you! I hate you! (*She throws the rope violently around the room. The phone stops ringing.*) Thank God. (*She looks at the stove, goes over to it, and turns the gas on. The sound of gas escaping is heard. Babe sniffs at it.*) Come

67

on. Come on...Hurry up...I beg of you—hurry up! (*Finally, Babe feels the oven is ready; she takes a deep breath and opens the oven door to stick her head into it. She spots the rack and furiously jerks it out. Taking another breath, she sticks her head into the oven. She stands for several moments tapping her fingers furiously on top of the stove. She speaks from inside the oven...*) Oh, please. Please. (*After a few moments, she reaches for the box of matches with her head still in the oven. She tries to strike a match. It doesn't catch.*) Oh, Mama, please! (*She throws the match away and is getting a second one.*) Mama... Mama...So that's why you done it! (*In her excitement she starts to get up, bangs her head and falls back in the stove. Meg enters from the back door, carrying a birthday cake in a pink box.*)

MEG. Babe! (*Meg throws the box down and runs to pull Babe's head out of the oven.*) Oh, my God! What are you doing? What the hell are you doing?

BABE. (*Dizzily.*) Nothing. I don't know. Nothing. (*Meg turns off the gas and moves Babe to a chair near the open door.*)

MEG. Sit down. Sit down! Will you sit down!

BABE. I'm okay. I'm okay.

MEG. Put your head between your knees and breathe deep!

BABE. Meg—

MEG. Just do it! I'll get you some water. (*Meg gets some water for Babe.*) Here.

BABE. Thanks.

MEG. Are you okay?

BABE. Uh-huh.

MEG. Are you sure?

BABE. Yeah, I'm sure. I'm okay.

MEG. (*Getting a damp rag and putting it over her own face.*) Well good. That's good.

BABE. Meg—

MEG. Yes?

BABE. I know why she did it.

MEG. What? Why who did what?

BABE. (*With joy.*) Mama. I know why she hung that cat along with her.

MEG. You do?

BABE. (*With enlightenment.*) It's 'cause she was afraid of dying all alone.

MEG. Was she?

BABE. She felt so unsure, you know, as to what was coming. It seems the best thing coming up would be a lot of angels and all of them singing. But I imagine they have high, scary voices and little gold pointed fingers that are as sharp as blades and you don't want to meet 'em all alone. You'd be afraid to meet 'em all alone. So it wasn't like what people were saying about her hating that cat. Fact is, she loved that cat. She needed him with her 'cause she felt so all alone.

MEG. Oh, Babe . . . . Babe. Why, Babe? Why?

BABE. Why what?

MEG. Why did you stick your head into the oven?!

BABE. I don't know, Meg. I'm having a bad day. It's been a real bad day; those pictures; and Barnette giving up his vendetta; then Willie Jay, heading north; and—Zackery called me up. (*Trembling with terror.*) He says he's gonna have me classified insane and send me on out to the Whitfield asylum.

MEG. What! Why, he could never do that!

BABE. Why not?

MEG. 'Cause you're not insane.

BABE. I'm not?

MEG. No! He's trying to bluff you. Don't you see it? Barnette's got him running scared.

BABE. Really?

MEG. Sure. He's scared to death—calling you insane. Ha! Why, you're just as perfectly sane as anyone walking the streets of Hazlehurst, Mississippi.

BABE. I am?

MEG. More so! A lot more so!

BABE. Good!

MEG. But, Babe, we've just got to learn how to get through these real bad days here. I mean, it's getting to be a thing in our family. (*Slight pause as she looks at Babe.*) Come on now. Look, we've got Lenny's cake right here. I mean don't you wanna be around to give her her cake; watch her blow out the candles?

BABE. (*Realizing how much she wants to be here.*) Yeah, I do, I do. Cause she always loves to make her birthday wishes on those candles.

MEG. Well, then we'll give her her cake and maybe you won't be so miserable.

BABE. Okay.

MEG. Good. Go on and take it out of the box.

BABE. Okay. (*She takes the cake out of the box. It is a magical moment.*) Gosh, it's a pretty cake.

MEG. (*Handing her some matches.*) Here now. You can go on and light up the candles.

BABE. All right. (*She starts to light the candles.*) I love to light up candles. And there are so many here. Thirty pink ones in all plus one green one to grow on.

MEG. (*Watching her light the candles.*) They're pretty.

BABE. They are. (*She stops lighting the candles.*) And I'm not like Mama. I'm not so all alone.

MEG. You're not.

BABE. (*As she goes back to lighting candles.*) Well, you'd better keep an eye out for Lenny. She's supposed to be surprised.

MEG. All right. Do you know where she's gone?

BABE. Well, she's not here inside—so she must have gone on outside.

MEG. Oh, well, then I'd better run and find her.

BABE. Okay 'cause these candles are gonna melt down. (*Meg starts out the door.*)

MEG. Wait—there she is coming. Lenny! Oh, Lenny! Come on! Hurry up!

BABE. (*Overlapping and improvising as she finishes lighting candles.*) Oh, no! No! Well, yes—yes! No, wait! Wait! Okay! (*Lenny enters. Meg covers Lenny's eyes with her hands.*)

LENNY. (*Terrified.*) What?! What is it?!! What?!!

MEG & BABE. Surprise! Happy Birthday! Happy Birthday to Lenny!!

LENNY. Oh, no! Oh me!!! What a surprise! I could just cry!

Oh, look, "Happy Birthday to Lenny—A Day Late!" How cute! My! Will you look at all those candles—it's absolutely frightening.

BABE. (*Spontaneous thought.*) Oh, no, Lenny, it's good! 'Cause —'cause the more candles you have on your cake, the stronger your wish is.

LENNY. Really?

BABE. Sure!

LENNY. Mercy. (*They start the song. Lenny, interrupting the song.*) Oh, but wait! I—I can't think of my wish! My body's gone all nervous inside.

MEG. For God's sake, Lenny—come on!

BABE. The wax is all melting!

LENNY. My mind is just a blank, a total blank!

MEG. Will you please just—

BABE. (*Overlapping.*) Lenny, hurry! Come on!

LENNY. Okay! Okay! Just go!! (*Meg and Babe burst into the "Happy Birthday Song." As it ends Lenny blows out all of the candles on the cake. Meg and Babe applaud loudly.*)

MEG. Oh, you made it!

BABE. Hurray!

LENNY. Oh, me! Oh, me! I hope that wish comes true! I hope it does!

BABE. Why? What did you wish for?

LENNY. (*As she removes the candles from the cake.*) Why. I can't tell you that.

BABE. Oh, sure you can—

LENNY. Oh, no! Then it won't come true.

BABE. Why, that's just superstition! Of course it will, if you made it deep enough.

MEG. Really? I didn't know that.

LENNY. Well, Babe's the regular expert on birthday wishes.

BABE. It's just I get these feelings. Now come on and tell us. What was it you wished for?

MEG. Yes, tell us. What was it?

LENNY. Well, I guess, it wasn't really a specific wish. This— this vision just sort of came into my mind.

BABE. A vision? What was it of?

LENNY. I don't know exactly. It was something about the three of us smiling and laughing together.

BABE. Well, when was it? Was it far away or near?

LENNY. I'm not sure, but it wasn't forever; it wasn't for every minute. Just this one moment and we were all laughing.

BABE. What were we laughing about?

LENNY. I don't know. Just nothing I guess.

MEG. Well, that's a nice wish to make. (*Lenny and Meg look at each other a moment.*) Here, now, I'll get a knife so we can go ahead and cut the cake in celebration of Lenny being born!

BABE. Oh, yes! And give each one of us a rose. A whole rose apiece!

LENNY. (*Cutting the cake nervously.*) Well, I'll try—I'll try!

MEG. (*Licking the icing off a candle.*) Mmmm—this icing is delicious! Here, try some!

BABE. Mmmm! It's wonderful! Here, Lenny!

LENNY. (*Laughing joyously as she licks icing from her fingers and cuts huge pieces of cake that her sisters bite into ravenously.*) Oh, how I do love having birthday cake for breakfast! How I do! (*The sisters freeze for a moment laughing and catching cake; the lights change and frame them in a magical, golden, sparkling glimmer; saxophone music is heard. The lights dim to blackout, and the saxophone continues to play.*)

END OF PLAY

PROPERTY INVENTORY

NOTE: All Bold Face Props are practical, all others are dressing or supplies.

PLACEMENT DESCRIPTION

Down Right Upper Shelves
Top shelf:
    5 quart jars with lids
    2 pint jars with lids
    2 small jars with lids
Second shelf:
    2 quart jars of Cheerio's
    1 pint jar of nuts
    1 pint jar of barley
    1 pint jar of rice
    1 pint jar of beans
Third shelf:
    Crock with lid
    1 pint jar of beans
    1 pint jar of noodles
    1 pint jar with lid
    1 small jar of nuts
    1 small jar of beans
Bottom shelf:
    Green coffee grinder
    Flour sifter
    Coffee pot
    Flowered metal cake box
    2 Revere ware pans

Hanging below:
    Egg beater

Down Right Hanging On Wall
Spice ice rack with 12 spice jars

Down Right Lower Shelves
Top shelf:
    Cardinal ceramic planter
    Spice rack with 10 spice jars
    Basket with 9 assorted salt and pepper shakers and small
        blue vase
    Grinder blades
    White flowered ceramic salt and pepper
    Glass salt and pepper
    Mr. and Mrs. Chef salt and pepper
    Black cast iron good luck trivet
    Grinder
Second shelf:
    Pan lid
    Utility scale
    Mr. Bear cookie jar
    Metal teapot
    Pan lid
Third shelf:
    Steam iron
    Green glass juicer
    Tin funnel
    Blue spouted mixing bowl
    White ceramic baby shoe planter
Bottom shelf:
    2 kettles with lids

Down Right Window
Hanging left:
    5 assorted pot holders
On sill:
    28 oz. carton Diamond Crystal salt

1 quart measuring cup
1 2 cup measuring cup
Hanging right:
   Cloth pot holder caddy with pot holders
STOVE
   OVEN RACK
   COFFEE POT
   Yellow kitten ceramic spoon rest
   BOX OF WOODEN KITCHEN MATCHES
   BLUE FLOWERED CHINA ASHTRAY
   BROWN FLOWERED POT HOLDER
   YELLOW STONEWARE CUP AND SAUCER
Over Doorway
   Electric fan
   Orange insecticide sprayer
   3 metal tea boxes
On Porch
   Six foot step ladder
   STRAW BROOM
   BLACK METAL DUSTPAN
   Wall thermometer
   2 small baskets (inside bushel basket)
   2 carpet beaters
   2 white towels
   Orange insecticide sprayer
   Pink throw rug
Downstage Side of Cupboard
   Pennsylvania Dutch cheese board
   1974 calendar
   HOOK FOR KEYS

Up Right Cupboard
On top:
   Red and white flowered metal breadbox
   3 Happy Chef canisters
Top left cupboard
   Empty
Bottom left cupboard

Top shelf:
    White china soup tureen
    2 16 oz. Mueller's noodles
    48 oz. can Crisco shortening
    32 oz. pkg. Aunt Jemima corn meal mix
    2 12 oz. boxes Quaker instant oatmeal
    2 16 oz. boxes Premium saltines
Second shelf:
    4 glasses: amber with roses
    48 oz. Carolina rice
    Box Tender Leaf tea: 100 bags
    12 oz. can Davis baking powder
    10 oz. jar Nescafe instant coffee
    5 lb. pkg. Waldbaum's sugar
    5 lb. pkg. Gold Medal flour
    32 oz. box Presto cake flour
    10 oz. box Nabisco Shredded Wheat
    6 oz. box Kellogg's Rice Krispies
    12 oz. box Post Grape Nuts Flakes
    Flowered fabric backing
Bottom shelf:
    White china pear plate
    China serving bowl
    8 stoneware salad plates
    16 oz. can Redpack tomatoes
    16 oz. box Arm & Hammer baking soda
    26 oz. carton Diamond Crystal salt
    3 16 oz. cans Libby's beets
    Box Glad straws: 40 straws
    2 16 oz. cans Del Monte green beans
    2 16 oz. cans Del Monte corn
    16 oz. can S & W cream style corn
    12 oz. can Del Monte corn
    3 16 oz. cans King Cole carrots
    40 oz. box Bisquick
    Flowered fabric backing
Tacked on upstage door:
    3 Recipe cards

Up Right Counter
BLUE METAL LEAF ASHTRAY
6 white metal canisters with red lids
   in MEDIUM CANNISTER
     SUGAR
     SMALL METAL SCOOP
WODDEN FRUIT BOWL
   4 LEMONS
   2 APPLES
   2 Oranges
Mixmaster with bowls, beaters, and juicer attachment

Up Right Drawers
Downstage drawer:
   SCISSORS
   JAR OF RUBBER CEMENT
   4½" HAIR RIBBONS
   8 STICK ON BOWS
   2 LARGE SPOOLS THREAD
   2 SMALL SPOOLS THREAD
   2 SIZE D BATTERIES
   4 PKGS. SHOELACES
   3' LENGTH ¼" COTTON CLOTHESLINE
   1 BALL STRING
   3' LENGTH TWINE
   6' LENGTH TWINE
   2 PKGS. HALLMARK GIFT TYE
   10' LENGTH ½" RED DRAPERY CORD
Upstage drawer:
(This drawer has been dressed but is never opened.)
   2 boxes Reynold's Wrap 75'
   2 boxes Lady Dianne Plasticware
   Paring knife
   Box Glad straws: 40 straws
   Box Saran wrap 50'
   Scotch tape dispenser
   4 pkgs. small note cards 1½ x 3
   DULL KNIFE: 10" BUTCHER KNIFE

Up Right Center Drawers
Left drawer:
(This drawer has been dressed but is never opened.)
BOX GLAD DISPOSER SIZE TRASH BAGS
2 Boxes Ball zinc caps: 12 ea.
2 Large slotted spoons
15" Serrated knife (BACK UP)
3 BOXES DIAMOND KITCHEN MATCHES

Up Right Bottom Cupboards
Empty

Up Right Cupboard
Top right cupboard:
pie pan
Black metal Massachussetts tray
BLACK POPCORN POT
Bottom right cupboard:
Top shelf:
6 glasses: amber with roses
4 stoneware plates
6 stoneware saucers
Second shelf:
5 aluminum glasses
3 stoneware plates
4 stoneware salad plates
Bottom shelf:
11 stoneware soup bowls
4 stoneware salad plates
GLASS FLOWERED LEMONADE PITCHER
2 stoneware plates
4 frosted glasses

Up Center Window
2 green window shades
Hanging light fixture
2 wall brackets with hanging plants
Metal plant holder with potted plant

Ceramic dolphin placque
Metal basket with bar of Ivory soap
On sill:
Ceramic donkey cart with plant
Ceramic clown/pig with plant
Small hurricane lamp
China doll figurine
Ceramic cradle with plant
EARTHENWARE POT WITH PLANT
At right:
KNIFE RACK
KNIFE
CAKE KNIFE: 10" BUTCHER KNIFE
Hanging outside:
Birch birdhouse

Up Center Counter
At left:
Yellow metal napkin box
Glass plant sprayer
22 OZ. BOTTLE IVORY SOAP
GREEN PLASTIC DRAINER AND CUSHION
2 GLASSES: AMBER WITH ROSES
4 JUICE GLASSES: FLOWERED
SINK
WASHRAG
At right:
WOODEN PAPER TOWEL RACK WITH YELLOW PAPER
   TOWELS
WHITE LINEN DISHTOWEL
Thermos bottle
PINK LINEN DISHTOWEL
Below sink:
FLOWERED CURTAIN ON STRING
GREEN METAL WASTEBASKET WITH LINER
At left:
22 oz. Bottle Windex
14 oz. can Ajax powder

32 oz. bottle Woolite
28 oz. bottle Mr. Clean
28 oz. bottle Ajax liquid
At right:
    16 oz. can Raid

Up Left Center
WOODEN KITCHEN STEP STOOL

Up Right Center Drawers
Right drawer:
    BOX OF BOOK MATCHES
    Box Ziploc storage bags: 20 gal. size
    2 boxes Glad sandwich bags: 17 bags ea.

Up Center China Cupboard
Hanging above:
    Large white flowered china platter
Top shelf:
    China lemons relish tray
    Set of china: 3 plates, 12 salad plates, 4 bowls
    Brown serving crock
On hooks:
    4 stoneware cups
Hanging below:
    White metal Florida tray
    Glass pitcher
    2 glass cruets
    Glass salt and pepper
    Glass sugar bowl and creamer
    5 flowered juice glasses
    4 GLASSES: AMBER WITH ROSES
On counter:
    Glass vase
    White metal Fruit tray
    Nut chopper jar
    Ceramic hot plate
    Brass baby shoe

CERAMIC GRANDMA COOKIE JAR
ARCHWAY BIG CHIP CHOCOLATE CHIP COOKIES
On front of counter:
STARR WALL-MOUNTED BOTTLE OPENER

Up Center Drawers
Left drawer:
(This drawer has been dressed but is never opened.)
   Miscellaneous kitchen utensils
Right drawer:
(This drawer has been dressed but is never opened.)
   Linen towels

Up Center Lower Shelves
Top shelf:
   5 bars Ivory soap
   2 pkgs. cellulose sponges 4 ea.
   2 15 oz. cans Ann Page black-eyed peas
   12 oz. can Del Monte corn
   2 16 oz. cans Ann Page mixed vegetables
   2 28 oz. cans Red Pack tomatoes
   4 cans Campbell tomato soup
   2 16 oz. cans Green Giant green beans
   1 16 oz. can Libby's beets
   46 oz. can Dole pineapple juice
   46 oz. can Sacramento tomato juice
   3 16 oz. cans Heinz pork 'n' beans
   Metal basket
Bottom shelf:
   Wooden salad bowl
   Ceramic apple cookie jar
   5 metal cups
   Ceramic pink scallop candy dish

Up Center Shelves
Top shelf:
   White china rose vase
   White china autumn leaves pitcher

Red ceramic vase
Green flowered decorative fan
Yellow and blue ceramic planter
Hanging above second shelf:
   3 stoneware plates
Second shelf:
   2 white ceramic rose candle holders
   2 white china flowered tureens with lids
Hanging from second shelf:
   4 white china flowered cups
Bottom shelf:
   White tatted doily
   Green ceramic urn
   White flowered china gravy boat
   Yellow flowered china sugar bowl and creamer
   Ceramic squirrel salt and pepper
   Ceramic duck planter

Up Center Wall
Hanging below shelves:
   Plastic cottage thermometer/barometer
   Flowered ceramic tile

REFRIGERATOR
On top:
   Electric broiler toaster oven
   White flowered embroidered table scarf
On door:
   Recipe card
   4 magnetic fruit stickers
Top shelf:
   Bag of apples (storage)
   Bag of oranges (storage)
Second shelf:
   4 7½ OZ. COKES
   Quart of milk
   Bag of apples (storage)

Third shelf:
   16 oz. box Arm & Hammer baking soda
   32 oz. jar Hellman's mayonnaise
   16 oz. bottle Karo dark syrup
   8 oz. bottle Gulden's spicy brown mustard
   32 oz. bottle Ann Page spaghetti sauce
   China bowl covered with foil
Fourth shelf:
   China plate covered with foil
Bottom shelf:
   46 oz. can Dole pineapple juice
   14 oz. bottle Heinz ketchup
   46 oz. can Sacramento tomato juice
   2 12 oz. jars Kretchsmer wheat germ
   Bag of lemons (storage)

In freezer
Top shelf:
   Ice cube tray
Bottom shelf:
   PLASTIC BOWL OF ICE CUBES

Up Left Center Shelves
Top shelf:
   White flowered china sugar bowl
   Green flowered ceramic vase
   Small leather covered box
   Wooden box
   Shell fish figurine
Second shelf:
   Wide mouthed jar filled with plastic game pieces and stick
      on bows
   Blue ceramic vase
   Ceramic pig planter
   Gold cast iron Liberty Bell bookends
   Yahtzee game box
Third shelf:
   5 assorted books

Monopoly game box
Parcheesi game board
Box of 28 dominoes
Blue plasic dice cup
Inlaid wooden box
Yahtzee score pad
Scrabble crossword game box
Bingo deluxe edition game box
Brocade fringe
Fourth shelf:
Small green metal tray
Black metal covered candy dish
RUBBER BANDED DECK OF CARDS
Small clasp Bible
Glass candy dish
Ceramic cactus salt and pepper
Metal apple preserves pot with lid
Fifth shelf:
Silver cast iron napkin holder
Rubber banded deck of cards (BACK UP)
Red ceramic horse figurine
Green ceramic candle holder
2 glass bottles with decorative trim
Bottom shelf:
Frosted glass pineapple pitcher
Coffee pot
Wooden preserves tray with 2 glass bowls and wooden lids

Up Left Center Stairs
Green flowered carpet runner
Red flowered carpet runner

Up Left Center Telephone Shelf
BLACK STANDARD TELEPHONE WITH
    METAL DAIL & 12' CORD
Braided rag doily
COPIAH COUNTY PHONE DIRECTORY

3" x 5 NOTE PAD
PENCIL

Up Left Center Newel Post
Wall sconce
Letter organizer with recipe note cards

Up Left Wall
Yellow ceramic plate
Set of shelves
   Top shelf:
      White flowered china pitcher
      White cornucopia china vase
      Yellow ceramic chicken figurine
   Bottom shelf:
      White flowered china vase
      Ceramic dog planter
      Flamingo palm tree shell souvenir
God Bless Our Garden plate

Stage Left Bay Window
2 green window shades
On window seat:
   4 assorted throw pillows
   Small black electric fan
   Plastic wicker sewing basket
   White alarm clock

Stage Left Center
ROLLAWAY COT:
   Flowered sheets
   Blue flowered spread
   Brown flowered cover
   PILLOW WITH BROWN FLOWERED PILLOWCASE
Brown flowered hooked rug

Stage Right Center
ENAMEL TOPPED KITCHEN TABLE WITH DRAWER
In drawer:
3 drawer organizer trays
1: ALLIGATOR NUTCRACKER
SHARP 12" SERRATED KNIFE
2: Nutcracker (BACK UP)
6 pcs. assorted silverware
3 WOODEN KITCHEN CHAIRS

Up Center Landing
Blue flowered rug

Up Left Center Dining Room
Sideboard:
Crocheted table scarf
White flowered china vase
Pink ceramic scallop vase with plant
2 white flowered china creamers
On shelf below:
White flowered china platter
White flowered china bowl
Red metal silent butler
Beige and gold metal wastebasket

Up Center Arbor
Artificial rose vines
Artificial grass
Artificial bushes
2 artificial trees

Stage Left Window Backing
Artificial tree
Artificial bushes
Artificial rose vines
Artificial grass
Artificial hedge

Hanging over Table
  Brass chandelier with four fluted lamps

On up Left Stairway Wall
  Wall sconce with glass shade

OFFSTAGE HAND PROPS AND SUPPLIES

LENNY:
SET OF KEYS ON PAPERCLIP WIRE KEY RING
9 X 12" PAPER SACK
PKG. BLUE TWILITE LARGE SPIRAL CANDLES
PKG. BEIGETONE MEDIUM NATIONAL BRAND
   SECONDS SUPPORT PANTY HOSE
PINK SUITCASE dressed with clothing
PHOTO ALBUM WITH:
   WEDDING PICTURE
   MEG SINGING AT GREENY'S PICTURE
   JIMMY CLOWNING AT THE BEACH 1952 PICTURE
   MAMA AND THE CAT PICTURE
ALTO SAXOPHONE WITH CASE, MOUTHPIECE COVER
   AND REEDS

CHICK:
13 OZ. BOX ALL SOFT CENTERS WHITMAN'S CANDY
BLUE AND PINK NURSERY GIFTWRAP
2 X 3" GIFT CARD/23 X 12" POINSETTIA CELLOPHANE
   STRIPS
SET OF KEYS ON SMALL RING WITH PLASTIC TAB
8½ X 11 TWO COLUMN LIST OF RELATIVES
   AND PHONE NUMBERS

DOC:
#8 BROWN PAPER BAG (8 X 16") DOUBLE BAGGED
   AND FILLED WITH UNSHELLED PECANS

MEG:

MARLBORO CIGARETTE BOX WITH SUBSTITUTION
OF HONEY ROSE FILTER-TIPPED
HERBAL CIGARETTES
BIC LIGHTER
Bic lighter (BACK UP)
TOOTHBRUSH
3 OZ. TUBE GLEEM TOOTHPASTE
COPIAH COUNTY COURIER NEWSPAPER WITH
"SHOOTING AT BOTRELLE MANSION; SENATOR IN
CRITICAL CONDITION" HEADLINE
500 ML BOTTLE JIM BEAM BLACK LABEL BOURBON
(CARAMEL COLORED WATER)
HAIRBRUSH
BOTTLE OF EMPIRIN WITH PLASTIC SNAP-ON CAP
(SUBSTITUTE VITAMIN C)
4" POCKET MIRROR
½ OZ. BOTTLE MURINE EYE DROPS
18½ X 28" CARDBOARD CAKE BOX
18 X 26" MASONITE CAKE BASE BOARD
16 X 25" ARTIFICIAL CAKE: CHOCOLATE WITH WHITE
ICING RED ROSETTES, AND RED LETTERING—
"HAPPY BIRTHDAY LENNY A DAY LATE"
4½ X 14½ SECTION OF PRACTICAL CAKE
WITH THREE ROSETTES
30 PINK TWILIGHT SMALL SPIRAL CANDLES
AND CANDLEHOLDERS
1 GREEN TWILITE LARGE SPIRAL CANDLE
AND CANDLEHOLDER
6" WHITE PAPER DOILIES

BABE:

PINK COSMETIC CASE
PINK DRAWSTRING CURLER BAG
PINK HAIRBRUSH

12 PINK FOAM CURLERS
Cosmetics
Lingerie
BROKEN NOOSE WITH BREAKAWAY KNOT

BARNETTE:
   3⅝ X 6½" WHITE ENVELOPE
   5:3 ⅜ X 4¼" BLACK & WHITE POLAROID
     SEX PICTURES
     (BLACK MAN/WHITE WOMAN)
   2 X 3" CALLING CARD: BARNETTE LLOYD
     "ATTORNEY AT LAW" WITH PHONE NUMBER
     AND ADDRESS
   BROWN LEATHER BRIEFCASE WITH SPRING CLASPS
   LETTER-SIZE FILE FOLDER
   3 PAGE MEDICAL CHART
   LEGAL PAD WITH NOTES
   2 PENCILS

   3 DAMP HAND TOWELS
   SMALL ALUMINUM SAUCEPAN
   TABLESPOON
   STONEWARE BOWL
   TEASPOON
   INSTANT QUAKER OATMEAL RAISIN AND SPICE
     FLAVOR (8 1½ OZ. PKGS. PER BOX)
   CINNAMON
   MILK
   STONEWARE CUP AND SAUCER
   BOX OF PRE-BURNT KITCHEN MATCHES
   Lemonade pitcher (BACK UP)

SUPPLIES:
   Rubbermaid plastic dishpan
   2 cup electric hot pot
   Mr. Coffee coffee maker with filters and COFFEE

36" straight-edge metal ruler
¾" scotch tape
Scissors
Large metal spatula
Cool whip
Kitchen fork
Paper towels
Kleenex
Paper cups
Backstage water pitcher
Backstage mirror
Terrycloth towels
Backstage refrigerator for storage
2 prop tables: 1 16 x 36" for hand props; 1 20 x 96" for work
  space
DOOR SLAM
HEAVY WOODEN CHAIR FOR SUICIDE SOUND EFFECT
SMALL BLOCK OF WOOD ON STRING FOR SCREEN
  DOOR KNOCKER
2 equity cots

PROP PRE-SET PLACEMENT

STOVE
In oven (above second slot)
   OVEN RACK
On back right burner
   COFFEE POT
   in pot:
   COFFEE (2½ cups)
   On stove top:
   SPOON REST
   BOX OF MATCHES
   ASHTRAY
   POT HOLDER
   CUP, SAUCER
On porch:
   BROOM
   DUSTPAN
On stage right counter:
   3 CANISTERS
      in medium canister:
         SUGAR
         SCOOP
   ASHTRAY
   FRUITBOWL
      in bowl:
         4 LEMONS
         2 APPLES
         2 ORANGES
In first drawer:
   RUBBER CEMENT
   SCISSORS

RED ROPE
(RIBBONS, TWINE, BOWS, THREAD)
In top up right cupboard:
POPCORN POT
In lower up right cupboard—bottom shelf:
LEMONADE PITCHER
On up right counter:
DISH DRAINER
in drainer:
2 TUMBLERS
4 GLASSES
SOAP BOTTLE
In drawer left of sink:
BOOK MATCHES

SINK
Between spigot and left handle:
WASHRAG
Under sink:
WASTEBASKET
in wastebasket:
LINER
In rack right of sink:
KNIFE
On window sill right of sink:
POTTED PLANT
In towel rack:
PAPER TOWELS
On counter right of sink:
TOWEL
Over drawer knob right of sink:
TOWEL
In glass front cupboard—bottom shelf at right:
3 TUMBLERS
On counter next to fridge:
COOKIE JAR
in jar:
LARGE COOKIES

KITCHEN STEPSTOOL

REFRIGERATOR
in freezer:
   PLASTIC BOWL
     in bowl:
     ICE CUBES
on second shelf at left:
   BOTTLE OF COKE (cap loosened)
On stairway shelf in covered dish:
   DECK OF CARDS
Over banister:
   LENNY'S COAT
On telephone cabinet:
   TELEPHONE (wire coiled)
   PHONE BOOK
   PAD
   PENCIL

COT
on cot:
   SPREAD
   PILLOW

TABLE
   in drawer:
     NUTCRACKER
     SHARP KNIFE

3 CHAIRS

OFFSTAGE PROP TABLE
LENNY:
   PURSE
   KEYS
   SACK

in sack:
PACKAGE OF CANDLES (cellophane slit)
PACKAGE OF PANTYHOSE (pre-opened)
SUITCASE
in case:
PHOTO ALBUM
(CLOTHING)
SAX CASE
in case:
SAXOPHONE
MOUTHPIECE COVER
REED

CHICK:
PURSE
in purse:
HAIR BRUSH
BOX OF CANDY
with:
GIFT WRAP
NOTECARD
KEYS
LIST OF RELATIVES

DOC:
BAG OF PECANS

MEG:
PURSE
in purse:
CIGARETTES (Marlboro box substitute Barclay's)
BIC LIGHTER
TOOTHPASTE
TOOTHBRUSH
NEWSPAPER
BOTTLE OF BOURBON (seal broken: ¾ full)
BROKEN HEEL

TOTEBAG
  in bag—left pocket
  BRUSH
  BOTTLE OF EMPIRIN
  in bag—right pocket
  COSMETIC BAG
   in bag:
    MURINE
    MIRROR

BABE:
 PURSE
 OVERNIGHT CASE
 in case:
  CURLER BAG
  in bag:
   CURLERS
   BRUSH
  (COSMETICS)
  (LINGERIE)

BARNETTE:
 ENVELOPE
 in envelope:
  SEX PICTURES
  CALLING CARD
 BRIEFCASE
 in case:
  FOLDER
  in folder:
   3-PAGE CHART
  LEGAL PAD
  PENCIL

CAKE BOX

in box:
    CAKE
    with:
        REAL CAKE PLUG
        CANDLES
    WATER PITCHER
    CUPS
    KLEENEX
    DOORSLAM
    BREAKAWAY NOOSE
    CHAIR

ACT II PRE-SET

STOVE
    on front left burner:
    PAN
        in pan:
        OATMEAL
        SPOON
    on back right burner:
    COFFEE POT
        in pot:
        COFFEE (7 cups)
    on stove top:
        (SPOON REST)
        (BOX OF MATCHES)
        (ASHTRAY)
        CUP, SAUCER
        POT HOLDER
    On up right counter:
        DISH DRAINER
        in drainer:
            (2 TUMBLERS)

4 GLASSES
Over bannister:
  BABE'S COAT
On telephone cabinet:
  TELEPHONE (wire coiled)
  PHONE BOOK
  PAD
  PENCIL
At foot of telephone cabinet:
  TOTE BAG
On stairway:
  SWEATER
Stage left of stairway seat:
  SUITCASE
  OVERNIGHT CASE
On window seat—downstage:
  SAX CASE (open)
  in case:
    SAXOPHONE (set up)
COT
on cot—up right corner:
  CANDY
under cot—up right corner:
  BABE'S SHOES

TABLE
on table:
  PAD
  PENCIL
  BRIEFCASE
  in case:
    FOLDER
    in folder:
      CHART
  ASHTRAY
  BOWL
  in bowl:
    OATMEAL

SPOON

3 CHAIRS
over back of center chair:
   BARNETTE'S JACKET

MEG:
   PURSE
   in purse:
      CIGARETTES
      LIGHTER
      (TOOTHPASTE)
      (TOOTHBRUSH)

ACT III PRE-SET

STOVE
   on stove top:
   (SPOON REST)
   (ASHTRAY)
   (POT HOLDER)
   BOX OF PRE-BURNT MATCHES
On counter right of sink:
   MEG'S PURSE
   in purse:
      CIGARETTES
      LIGHTER
      (TOOTHPASTE)
      (TOOTHBRUSH)
On shelf over fridge at left:
   ENVELOPE
   in envelope:
   SEX PICTURES

COT:
on cot:
   (PILLOW)

TOTE BAG
  in bag—left pocket:
    (BOTTLE OF EMPIRIN)
    BRUSH
  SAXOPHONE
under right corner of cot:
  PHOTO ALBUM

TABLE
in drawer:
  DULL KNIFE
  (NUTCRACKER)

3 CHAIRS

OFFSTAGE PROP TABLE

LENNY
  PURSE
  KEYS
  COAT

MEG
  UNBROKEN SHOE

  3 TOWELS

COSTUME PLOT

ACT I

LENNY
  Beige cardigan sweater
  Blue-grey cotton skirt
  Pink, blue & white blouse
  Beige corduroy tennies
  Beige full slip
  Pantyhose
  Barette
  Ecru handbag

MEG
  Plaid man's shirt
  Dk. teal blue mini skirt
  Black ankle strap heels
  Pantyhose
  Bra/gold necklace
  Bikinis-beige
  Black tap pants
  Black trenchcoat
  Wig
  Navy nylon travel bag
  Maroon purse

BABE
  White, pink, purple dress
  Rose leather belt

Beige sandals
Beige full slip
Pantyhose, briefs (beige)
Bra
Pink barette
Wedding & engagement rings
Opal & diamond ring
Gold heart necklace
Off white purse
Peach raincoat

CHICK
Orange white dress
Bone sling back shoes
Pantyhose-ripped
White half slip
Briefs-pink
Bra
Wedding & engagement rings
Gold watch
Necklace-painted wooden beads
Earrings
Bone handbag
Headband

BARNETTE
Beige 3 button 2 pc.
White suit
White shirt
Brown belt
Tie
Brown slip on shoes with gold buckles
Gold Timex watch
Crew neck T-shirt

DOC
Short sleeved beige, red, green plaid shirt

Beige chinos
Brown leather woven belt
Brown grey hush puppies
Camel knit socks
Gold wedding band
Gold watch
Yellow tractor hat
White handkerchief
White V neck T Shirt

ACT II

LENNY
   2 Pc dress—cream top, plaid skirt, plaid vest
   Navy flat shoes
   Pantyhose I
   Slip I
   Barette I, handbag I
   Blue raincoat

Change:
   Vest to sweater I
Change:
   To ACT I
MEG:
   Purple long-sleeved dress
   Shoes I
   Pantyhose I
   Bra I
   Bikinis I
   Tap pants I
   Coat I
   Wig I
   Purse I
   Necklace I

BABE
    Pink flowered satin robe
    Peach slippers
    Pantyhose, briefs I
    Slip I
    Bra I
    Barettes, jewelry I
    Remove robe
ADD:
    Raincoat I
Remove slippers, add
    Shoes I

BARNETTE
    Same as I
    Remove coat, roll up sleeves of shirt I
    Replace coat

DOC
    Blue plaid long-sleeved shirt
    Faded blue jeans
    Brown leather belt
    Brown work boots
    White athletic socks
    Jewelry I
    Handkerchief I
    Hat I
    T-Shirt I
    Beige poplin jacket

ACT III

LENNY
Same as I

MEG
    Same as II, Except:

Remove wig I, carry on wig II
Replace right shoe w/broken shoe
Replace broken shoe w/right shoe

BABE
Same as Act II (End)

CHICK
Blue flowered dress
Red flowered apron
Moccasins
Slip, briefs, Bra I
Rings I
Gold cross on chain
Earrings
Headband
Remove apron
Shoes I
Necklace I

BARNETTE
Same as I

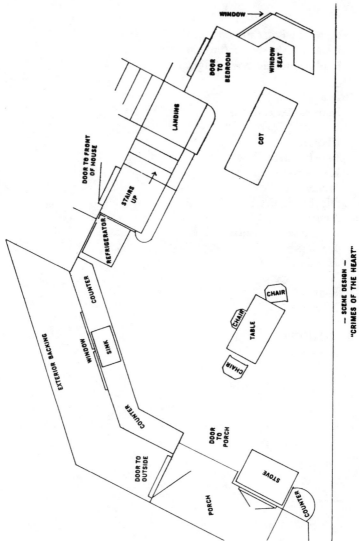

— SCENE DESIGN —
"CRIMES OF THE HEART"

NEW PLAYS

★ **THE EXONERATED by Jessica Blank and Erik Jensen.** Six interwoven stories paint a picture of an American criminal justice system gone horribly wrong and six brave souls who persevered to survive it. "The #1 play of the year...intense and deeply affecting..." –*NY Times.* "Riveting. Simple, honest storytelling that demands reflection." –*A.P.* "Artful and moving...pays tribute to the resilience of human hearts and minds." –*Variety.* "Stark...riveting...cunningly orchestrated." –*The New Yorker.* "Hard-hitting, powerful, and socially relevant." –*Hollywood Reporter.* [7M, 3W] ISBN: 0-8222-1946-8

★ **STRING FEVER by Jacquelyn Reingold.** Lily juggles the big issues: turning forty, artificial insemination and the elusive scientific Theory of Everything in this Off-Broadway comedy hit. "Applies the elusive rules of string theory to the conundrums of one woman's love life. Think *Sex and the City* meets *Copenhagen.*" –*NY Times.* "A funny offbeat and touching look at relationships...an appealing romantic comedy populated by oddball characters." –*NY Daily News.* "Where kooky, zany, and madcap meet...whimsically winsome." –*NY Magazine.* "STRING FEVER will have audience members happily stringing along." –*TheaterMania.com.* "Reingold's language is surprising, inventive, and unique." –*nytheatre.com.* "...[a] whimsical comic voice." –*Time Out.* [3M, 3W (doubling)] ISBN: 0-8222-1952-2

★ **DEBBIE DOES DALLAS adapted by Erica Schmidt, composed by Andrew Sherman, conceived by Susan L. Schwartz.** A modern morality tale told as a comic musical of tragic proportions as the classic film is brought to the stage. "A scream! A saucy, tongue-in-cheek romp." –*The New Yorker.* "Hilarious! DEBBIE manages to have it all: beauty, brains and a great sense of humor!" –*Time Out.* "Shamelessly silly, shrewdly self-aware and proud of being naughty. Great fun!" –*NY Times.* "Racy and raucous, a lighthearted, fast-paced thoroughly engaging and hilarious send-up." –*NY Daily News.* [3M, 5W] ISBN: 0-8222-1955-7

★ **THE MYSTERY PLAYS by Roberto Aguirre-Sacasa.** Two interrelated one acts, loosely based on the tradition of the medieval mystery plays. "... stylish, spine-tingling...Mr. Aguirre-Sacasa uses standard tricks of horror stories, borrowing liberally from masters like Kafka, Lovecraft, Hitchcock...But his mastery of the genre is his own...irresistible." –*NY Times.* "Undaunted by the special-effects limitations of theatre, playwright and *Marvel* comic-book writer Roberto Aguirre-Sacasa maps out some creepy twilight zones in THE MYSTERY PLAYS, an engaging, related pair of one acts...The theatre may rarely deliver shocks equivalent to, say, *Dawn of the Dead,* but Aguirre-Sacasa's work is fine compensation." –*Time Out.* [4M, 2W] ISBN: 0-8222-2038-5

★ **THE JOURNALS OF MIHAIL SEBASTIAN by David Auburn.** This epic one-man play spans eight tumultuous years and opens a uniquely personal window on the Romanian Holocaust and the Second World War. "Powerful." –*NY Times.* "[THE JOURNALS OF MIHAIL SEBASTIAN] allows us to glimpse the idiosyncratic effects of that awful history on one intelligent, pragmatic, recognizably real man..." –*NY Newsday.* [3M, 5W] ISBN: 0-8222-2006-7

★ **LIVING OUT by Lisa Loomer.** The story of the complicated relationship between a Salvadoran nanny and the Anglo lawyer she works for. "A stellar new play. Searingly funny." –*The New Yorker.* "Both generous and merciless, equally enjoyable and disturbing." –*NY Newsday.* "A bitingly funny new comedy. The plight of working mothers is explored from two pointedly contrasting perspectives in this sympathetic, sensitive new play." –*Variety.* [2M, 6W] ISBN: 0-8222-1994-8

DRAMATISTS PLAY SERVICE, INC.
440 Park Avenue South, New York, NY 10016 212-683-8960 Fax 212-213-1539
postmaster@dramatists.com www.dramatists.com

NEW PLAYS

★ **MATCH by Stephen Belber.** Mike and Lisa Davis interview a dancer and choreographer about his life, but it is soon evident that their agenda will either ruin or inspire them—and definitely change their lives forever. "Prolific laughs and ear-to-ear smiles." *–NY Magazine.* "Uproariously funny, deeply moving, enthralling theater. Stephen Belber's MATCH has great beauty and tenderness, and abounds in wit." *–NY Daily News.* "Three and a half out of four stars." *–USA Today.* "A theatrical steeplechase that leads straight from outrageous bitchery to unadorned, heartfelt emotion." *–Wall Street Journal.* [2M, 1W] ISBN: 0-8222-2020-2

★ **HANK WILLIAMS: LOST HIGHWAY by Randal Myler and Mark Harelik.** The story of the beloved and volatile country-music legend Hank Williams, featuring twenty-five of his most unforgettable songs. "[LOST HIGHWAY has] the exhilarating feeling of Williams on stage in a particular place on a particular night…serves up classic country with the edges raw and the energy hot…By the end of the play, you've traveled on a profound emotional journey: LOST HIGHWAY transports its audience and communicates the inspiring message of the beauty and richness of Williams' songs…forceful, clear-eyed, moving, impressive." *–Rolling Stone.* "…honors a very particular musical talent with care and energy… smart, sweet, poignant." *–NY Times.* [7M, 3W] ISBN: 0-8222-1985-9

★ **THE STORY by Tracey Scott Wilson.** An ambitious black newspaper reporter goes against her editor to investigate a murder and finds the *best* story…but at what cost? "A singular new voice…deeply emotional, deeply intellectual, and deeply musical…" *–The New Yorker.* "…a conscientious and absorbing new drama…" *–NY Times.* "…a riveting, tough-minded drama about race, reporting and the truth…" *–A.P.* "… a stylish, attention-holding script that ends on a chilling note that will leave viewers with much to talk about." *–Curtain Up.* [2M, 7W (doubling, flexible casting)] ISBN: 0-8222-1998-0

★ **OUR LADY OF 121st STREET by Stephen Adly Guirgis.** The body of Sister Rose, beloved Harlem nun, has been stolen, reuniting a group of life-challenged childhood friends who square off as they wait for her return. "A scorching and dark new comedy… Mr. Guirgis has one of the finest imaginations for dialogue to come along in years." *–NY Times.* "Stephen Guirgis may be the best playwright in America under forty." *–NY Magazine.* [8M, 4W] ISBN: 0-8222-1965-4

★ **HOLLYWOOD ARMS by Carrie Hamilton and Carol Burnett.** The coming-of-age story of a dreamer who manages to escape her bleak life and follow her romantic ambitions to stardom. Based on Carol Burnett's bestselling autobiography, *One More Time.* "…pure theatre and pure entertainment…" *–Talkin' Broadway.* "…a warm, fuzzy evening of theatre." *–BrodwayBeat.com.* "…chuckles and smiles of recognition or surprise flow naturally…a remarkable slice of life." *–TheatreScene.net.* [5M, 5W, 1 girl] ISBN: 0-8222-1959-X

★ **INVENTING VAN GOGH by Steven Dietz.** A haunting and hallucinatory drama about the making of art, the obsession to create and the fine line that separates truth from myth. "Like a van Gogh painting, Dietz's story is a gorgeous example of excess—one that remakes reality with broad, well-chosen brush strokes. At evening's end, we're left with the author's resounding opinions on art and artifice, and provoked by his constant query into which is greater: van Gogh's art or his violent myth." *–Phoenix New Times.* "Dietz's writing is never simple. It is always brilliant. Shaded, compressed, direct, lucid—he frames his subject with a remarkable understanding of painting as a physical experience." *–Tucson Citizen.* [4M, 1W] ISBN: 0-8222-1954-9

DRAMATISTS PLAY SERVICE, INC.
440 Park Avenue South, New York, NY 10016 212-683-8960 Fax 212-213-1539
postmaster@dramatists.com www.dramatists.com

NEW PLAYS

★ **INTIMATE APPAREL by Lynn Nottage.** The moving and lyrical story of a turn-of-the-century black seamstress whose gifted hands and sewing machine are the tools she uses to fashion her dreams from the whole cloth of her life's experiences. "…Nottage's play has a delicacy and eloquence that seem absolutely right for the time she is depicting…" –*NY Daily News.* "…thoughtful, affecting…The play offers poignant commentary on an era when the cut and color of one's dress—and of course, skin—determined whom one could and could not marry, sleep with, even talk to in public." –*Variety.* [2M, 4W] ISBN: 0-8222-2009-1

★ **BROOKLYN BOY by Donald Margulies.** A witty and insightful look at what happens to a writer when his novel hits the bestseller list. "The characters are beautifully drawn, the dialogue sparkles…" –*nytheatre.com.* "Few playwrights have the mastery to smartly investigate so much through a laugh-out-loud comedy that combines the vintage subject matter of successful writer-returning-to-ethnic-roots with the familiar mid-life crisis." –*Show Business Weekly.* [4M, 3W] ISBN: 0-8222-2074-1

★ **CROWNS by Regina Taylor.** Hats become a springboard for an exploration of black history and identity in this celebratory musical play. "Taylor pulls off a Hat Trick: She scores thrice, turning CROWNS into an artful amalgamation of oral history, fashion show, and musical theater…" –*TheatreMania.com.* "…wholly theatrical…Ms. Taylor has created a show that seems to arise out of spontaneous combustion, as if a bevy of department-store customers simultaneously decided to stage a revival meeting in the changing room." –*NY Times.* [1M, 6W (2 musicians)] ISBN: 0-8222-1963-8

★ **EXITS AND ENTRANCES by Athol Fugard.** The story of a relationship between a young playwright on the threshold of his career and an aging actor who has reached the end of his. "[Fugard] can say more with a single line than most playwrights convey in an entire script…Paraphrasing the title, it's safe to say this drama, making its memorable entrance into our consciousness, is unlikely to exit as long as a theater exists for exceptional work." –*Variety.* "A thought-provoking, elegant and engrossing new play…" –*Hollywood Reporter.* [2M] ISBN: 0-8222-2041-5

★ **BUG by Tracy Letts.** A thriller featuring a pair of star-crossed lovers in an Oklahoma City motel facing a bug invasion, paranoia, conspiracy theories and twisted psychological motives. "…obscenely exciting…top-flight craftsmanship. Buckle up and brace yourself…" –*NY Times.* "…[a] thoroughly outrageous and thoroughly entertaining play…the possibility of enemies, real and imagined, to squash has never been more theatrical." –*A.P.* [3M, 2W] ISBN: 0-8222-2016-4

★ **THOM PAIN (BASED ON NOTHING) by Will Eno.** An ordinary man muses on childhood, yearning, disappointment and loss, as he draws the audience into his last-ditch plea for empathy and enlightenment. "It's one of those treasured nights in the theater—treasured nights anywhere, for that matter—that can leave you both breathless with exhilaration and…in a puddle of tears." –*NY Times.* "Eno's words…are familiar, but proffered in a way that is constantly contradictory to our expectations. Beckett is certainly among his literary ancestors." –*nytheatre.com.* [1M] ISBN: 0-8222-2076-8

★ **THE LONG CHRISTMAS RIDE HOME by Paula Vogel.** Past, present and future collide on a snowy Christmas Eve for a troubled family of five. "…[a] lovely and hauntingly original family drama…a work that breathes so much life into the theater." –*Time Out.* "…[a] delicate visual feast…" –*NY Times.* "…brutal and lovely…the overall effect is magical." –*NY Newsday.* [3M, 3W] ISBN: 0-8222-2003-2

DRAMATISTS PLAY SERVICE, INC.
440 Park Avenue South, New York, NY 10016 212-683-8960 Fax 212-213-1539
postmaster@dramatists.com www.dramatists.com